Women in Transition

The Circle Book · A Year of Enrichment, Support and Sisterhood

52 Weeks of Material and Inspiration for Guiding Your Circle

Linda Laws

BALBOA.PRESS

A DIVISION OF HAY HOUSE

Balboa Press books may be ordered through booksellers or by contacting:

Balboa Press
A Division of Hay House
1663 Liberty Drive
Bloomington, IN 47403
www.balboapress.com
844-682-1282

ISBN: 978-1-9822-6135-1 (sc)
ISBN: 978-1-9822-6136-8 (e)

Library of Congress Control Number: 2021900608

Print information available on the last page.

Balboa Press rev. date: 01/20/2021

To George, for all the heart reasons, without whose encouragement
I may never have embarked upon that first circle journey.

We are one of the tens of thousands of women's circles that have sprung to life as the vehicles of change for the women committed to psycho-spiritual transformation. To that extent, we are living the visionary possibility that Women's Circles accelerate humanity's shift to a *post-patriarchal era*.

The extraordinary power of circles depends on a simple hypothesis ... that when a critical number of people change how they think and behave, the culture will change also, and a new era begins. Once the principles are understood, the significance of women's circles can be appreciated as a *revolutionary-evolutionary movement that is hidden in plain sight*.[1]

—Jean Shinoda Bolen, from *The Millionth Circle*

---

[1] Reproduced with permission from Jean Shinoda Bolen, *The Millionth Circle* (Berkeley, CA: Conari Press, 1999).

Contents

Fifty-Two Weeks of Material

Bringing a Circle to Its Final Close

Appendices

Preface

It is from a place of profound gratitude and inspiration that *Women in Transition* was conceived and brought into being, an offering to all the women who would like to form a women's circle, if only they had the syllabus to begin.

Presented in this book are fifty-two weeks of source material for facilitating a circle. Also included are guidelines for using a three-step process to bring a circle to its final close.

The material presented in these pages will provide a valuable foundation for your journey, whether you consult this book in your role as group leader or use it as a guide to implement your individual travels (see the afterward in the appendices).

The inquiries, meditations, and closing quotes can be used in any way you wish—as written, or as a springboard for your own circle journey ideas. They are offered as creative seeds, inspiration for the birth of new circles with the intention of connecting women with other women, locally and around the globe.

Acknowledgments

This book is a compilation from the more than five years of gatherings of an extraordinary group of women in an activity we call women's circles. The chronological time spent together was a fraction of the soul time we shared. The women we are today are infinitely more present, more actualized than our former selves, not only by virtue of having been immersed in a new way in which to communicate with ourselves and with one another but also by exposure to an entire community of women for whom this has become a way of being.

Three esteemed sources of guidance and inspiration for me in my tenure as facilitator of our circle came from the writings of Jean Shinoda Bolen, Clarissa Pinkola Estes, and Sue Patton Thoele, all veteran circle members and all staunch proponents of women's circles as powerful vehicles for change, interior and exterior.

I would like to extend my deepest, most heartfelt love and appreciation to the women with whom I traveled in this inexorable march toward the proverbial tipping point. In order of appearance, they are Renée, Karen, Reese, Tricia, Leenie, Holadia, Jillian, Elizabeth, and Jeannie, with special gratitude to my mentor, Willow. We took it beyond the furthest shores of imagination, my lovelies, and I thank you with all my heart.

Introduction

You will be teachers for each other. You will come together in Circles and speak your truth to each other. The time has come for women to accept their spiritual responsibility for the planet.[2]

—Sherry Ruth Anderson and Patricia Hopkins, *The Feminine Face of God*

Welcome to the extraordinary world of circles! Never has there been a time more conducive to the flourishing of women's circles. Women today have the means, the motive, and the opportunity to commune on a local and global scale. And while the benefits of circles are always delightfully piquant, they are also frequently unpredictable and unexpected. Much like the old adage, shake the chestnut tree, and the universe delivers mangoes, women who immerse themselves in the sisterhood of circle reap the harvest of a divine nature they could scarcely have imagined.

Women's circles come in many forms and guises. Some meet monthly in person, and some convene weekly on conference lines or audiovisual devices. Some circles exchange gifts, study common interests, cater to specific age groups, or study spiritual matters in preparation for self-transformation.

Regardless of their missions, the secret to all successful circles lies in creating a safe and comfortable vessel in which to travel together. Circle journeys weave a sacred web of intimate connection among their members and model the practice of speaking from the heart. We learn to withhold our judgments, respect one another's confidences, practice deep listening, and master the fine art of intentional speaking.

To sustain itself, a circle requires structural integrity. Ideally, the group's organization and the rules of the game are set forth up front and agreed upon by all members. Honoring these agreements, being authentically present, and doing one's own personal work (which can and will come up) all cultivate a climate ripe for discovery and change. Secrets are unveiled, paradigms shift and evolve, doors open, and choices are realized, all within the sacred womb of the circle.

I have been in women's circles for more than five years, and it has profoundly changed my life.

---

[2] Sherry Ruth Anderson and Patricia Hopkins, excerpt from *The Feminine Face of God* (New York, NY: Bantam Books, 1991).

Initially, my interest was in delving into my female nature, assuaging a restlessness that shrouded my own self-definition. I hungered for knowledge of my roots as told by the narrative of the sacred feminine.

Beyond simply finding a group of like-minded women, my circle experience introduced me to a sisterhood of souls who were consciously making choices, day by day, to embrace their highest potential, to illuminate their life's purpose and move into it. Along the way, we uncovered aspects of ourselves we had only vaguely intuited. Old, long-forgotten wounds rose to the surface for acknowledgment, forgiveness, and healing. Core issues shifted and resolved. A new sense of self-respect took deep root, and ultimately, a soul-level knowingness came into focus for each of us. The lessons that were ours, as individuals and as a group, were diverse and uniquely fitting. We could not have conceived of a better process.

Simply put, circle became a magnificent gift we each had bequeathed to ourselves and to one another.

The Genesis of a Circle

As individual women are drawn together in pursuit of a common intent, a sort of self-selection process seems to take place. From this organic coming together, the nature and complexion of that specific circle is born. The circle becomes an entity; call it group mind. It becomes the whole that is a composite of all its members. As an entity, this circle naturally gravitates toward a course that is determined by the interests, aptitudes, personalities, intentions, and capacities of these particular women to adventure and grow together. Everything flows from this.

The purpose or mission of the circle, its name, and its mode of conduct all arise from the pulse of the circle. Topics for the next meeting are determined by what happened in the meeting before, and so on. The journey shifts and evolves as the circle and its members shift and evolve. Nothing is predestined. To attune to this rhythm is to tap into the nature of creativity itself, so hold on to your knickers!

Considerations for Initiating a Circle

Circles thrive within a multiplicity of formats, and even ongoing groups reach plateaus during their process wherein change in orientation can benefit and stimulate new growth. As long as sanctity of the vessel itself is assured, options are limitless.

Consider the following points regarding purpose, organizational structure, and leadership styles. These primary topics are best defined at the inception of any new circle and should be in written form. They become the guiding documents for your circle and will assist you in staying on your intended course. Revisions to the guiding documents should not be undertaken lightly.

- Identify the intent of your circle. Write out that intention and provide each member with a copy. This can be a phrase, a statement of philosophy, or anything that helps define the main focus and goal of your group. The name of the circle may or may not be intrinsic to its purpose. A name may be selected by the founding members in advance, or you may wish to have the whole group participate in the naming process.

- Create guidelines for membership. Your guidelines clarify matters like expectations around attendance and timeliness, requirements for confidentiality, topics or activities considered inappropriate for your circle (religion, politics, promotion of personal business products or services), and any other rule of conduct you wish to encourage in your group. Write up the guidelines and provide a copy for each member. (See sample guidelines document in the appendices.)

- Establish the procedural protocol for the circle meeting itself. How often and how long will your circle meet? Where and when are the meetings? How many members are optimal, and what are the criteria for membership? What types of activities or topics for discussion support your purpose? What communication style(s) will you encourage as your circle's protocol? Will your circle's business best be accomplished by conversation, debate, storytelling, lecture, presentation, or quiet sharing?

- Define the role of leadership or facilitation style you believe would be optimal for your circle. A leadership position is best held for a predefined period of time—for instance, a month, three months, or a year. The role of leadership may be occupied by one person, shared by several members of the group, or may rotate. Note: It is well advised to change up leadership frequently enough so that no one member has the sole responsibility for leading the circle for an undue length of time. Overtaxing circle leadership will drain the energy of the entire circle.

- In conjunction with the type of leadership, also consider whether continuity of content may benefit your group. Circles providing an interconnected flow of topics from meeting to meeting create opportunities to plumb a subject more broadly and in greater depth. This often enhances and intensifies the growth process for each individual and for the group as a whole. On the other hand, increased diversity may better serve the needs and desires of the group.

The Critical Role of Facilitator

While being a member of a women's circle fosters a unique and fulfilling sense of belonging, intimacy, and expansion for all its members, the role of facilitator brings an added dimension of teacher and elder. She is responsible for consciously guiding the entire group along a chosen pathway.

A circle's leader is the wellspring for the lifeblood and spirit of the circle. While the colors and spice of the journey may flow directly from the diversity of the sisterhood as a whole, it is the facilitator who sets the vision and carries it safely aloft. Success requires clear intention, focus, and the ability to kindle and rekindle the flames of inspiration and commitment over time. The circle's leadership role has been likened to that of the shepherd of a flock: day by day, the well-being of each member and the group itself is gently watched over and nurtured by the facilitator.

Because of the importance of this position, some of the inner workings of this role are briefly discussed below.

The group's ongoing intention, guidelines, and continuity are carried by the facilitator. Each topic, each meditation, and the entire design and flow of circle meetings all align with the purpose of the circle. As the membership moves through individual and group dynamics—growth spurts, resistances, blocks, breakthroughs, evolutionary leaps—the facilitator must not only be mindful of these dynamics but also available to assist in the process. This may take the form of selecting topics that mirror and guide the movement of the group. She may connect with a member or members outside of the circle meeting to offer clarity or support. If the group has stalled or is experiencing an impasse, the facilitator may need to revisit the purpose or structure of the circle itself.

The senior members of the group provide a tremendous resource for the facilitator. Known as elder sisters, these women carry a wealth of information and experience useful in successfully charting the course for a circle. A facilitator may ask one or two elder sisters to work with her as assistants in facilitating the circle. This might include selecting meeting topics, identifying new projects or directions, guiding meditations, leading the meetings, and connecting one-on-one with members outside of the circle meeting.

Occupying the role of facilitator is one of the greatest gifts a circle has to offer its members. In striving to fulfill the needs of the group, a facilitator learns to access her own intuition, creativity, and leadership skills in new and deeply satisfying ways. As the circle's leader meets and successfully navigates the challenges of the journey, the work embraced by the circle evolves and transcends for the entire sisterhood.

While the attributes for successfully fulfilling the role of facilitator may seem daunting to a new member, over time and with exposure to the ongoing rhythm of the circle, they become at first familiar and then second nature to the membership. Eventually, most women begin to have a sense of how *they* would like to guide the circle. From this rise of individual creative preference comes the desire and intention to move into the leadership role.

Membership, Invitations and Attrition

The number of members in a circle will vary in direct relation to the purported mission of the circle. When identifying how many members is optimal for your circle, consider the matters of meeting time and place, time allotted for sharing and exchange among members, and the administrative tasks involved in running your circle.

Whether one is initiating a new circle or filling the vacancy of a departing member, the process of inviting a woman into your circle is paramount to maintaining the coherency of the group. There must be shared intentionality among sisters of a circle, a willingness to cohere with the circle's guiding documents while respecting the diversity within the group. The way in which the members hold and respect their circle determines the nature of that circle's journey. Without this common ground, the natural synergy of a circle ebbs away.

The initial interview with a prospective member is typically conducted by the facilitator, along with the member issuing the invitation and one or more elder sisters. The interview provides a venue in which to mutually share information about the circle experience, expectations for growth, and shared visions. A desirable candidate is then offered an opportunity to attend a circle meeting as a guest, a joint opportunity for the candidate and the membership to explore the fit.

If at some point it becomes apparent that the candidate does not feel like a natural fit for the group, it is the responsibility of the facilitator to bring those concerns back to the candidate. If the issue relates to timing or the availability to commit to the process, an otherwise desirable candidate may be encouraged to reconsider membership at a future time. A woman who clearly does not appear to fit with the group should be guided toward another more suitable choice.

The welcoming of a new member into the fold brings with it an excitement, a sense of anticipation and celebration of future travels together. Likewise, when the time comes for a seasoned member to take her leave from a circle, it can create a poignant opportunity to acknowledge that woman and the journey that has been shared together. Both transitions alter a circle. Establishing a ritual to honor these changes will assist in highlighting the positive aspects of change and will help move the group forward.

How One Circle Did It

The Circle of Deepening Light

Meetings of the Circle of Deepening Light were conducted on a telephone conference line. There were no visual distractions or interruptions during the call. Some of us never met in person or saw what one another looked like. The bonds created were born solely through voice and authentic sharing, a modus that forged deeply intimate and enduring connections.

Our circle name was decided upon by all the members. Because the group's interest was to seek illumination in exploring challenging intrapersonal topics to their deepest core, the group was strongly drawn to the idea of deepening light.

The statement of intention for this circle was "to live as women of the Light, with a high degree of integrity, fully committed to our own personal growth and spiritual awakening. To resolve and heal old blocks, to balance our feminine and masculine energies in a manner that promotes a life of love and abundance, and to empower others to do the same."

Leadership was shared by a facilitator and two elder sisters. These roles were initially held for one year.

The circle met weekly on Thursday evenings for one hour on a telephone conference line. Membership fluctuated between eight and nine members. Several days prior to the meeting, an inquiry was sent by the facilitator via email to each member. Inquiries typically were exercises or existential questions selected by the facilitator to expand the comfort zone and promote the growth of the sisterhood. Frequently, the inquiry would build upon a preceding inquiry or series of inquiries.

Each week's gathering commenced on time. The facilitator would welcome all the members to the call and immediately lead a brief meditation to settle the group and bring them to a state of mindfulness. The night's topic was reintroduced, and a figurative talking stick was placed in the center of the circle, to be taken up by whoever was first moved to share. This was called "picking up the talking stick." There was no order to member participation; as a member felt ready to speak, she would pick up the stick and take her turn.

Each sister's participation began with an offering of gratitude and mention of any breakthroughs she may have experienced during the week. She would then share what the inquiry evoked for her. At the end of her sharing, she would place the virtual talking stick back in the center for the next sister. The group acted as a listening witness to each sharing. Listening members were encouraged to mute their phones to reduce background noise. As a general rule, there were minimal or no interactive conversations during or after the sharing process. Oftentimes, what a sister shared during her turn was as much a revelation to her as it was to the group. And frequently, unexpected insights and unrealized emotions were unlocked during the sharing process, paving the way for healing and new growth.

While there was no specific time limit for individual sharing, the circle call itself was kept as close to sixty minutes as possible each week. This presumes the acknowledgment of an adequate portion of the hour for each member to speak. We found there was a natural ebb and flow among the members' needs to speak and be heard from week to week, and the call usually worked out to the hour. Typically, the facilitator would take her turn at the end of the evening and was able to adjust her sharing to the time remaining on the call. In the event of a time overrun, members were asked whether they would like to continue or if they preferred to excuse themselves from the call. From time to time, the facilitator gently reminded the group of the time parameters.

Following the general sharing of the whole group, the facilitator would read a quote or applicable poem to bring the evening to a close. If there was extra time, conversation among the general membership sometimes took place before saying good night. The usual feelings following a meeting were gratitude, a sense of expansiveness, and oftentimes wonder.

Summary

The intimacy and connection created by a circle of women who meet over an extended period of time can take your breath away.

The act of truly listening to someone and being listened to is transformative for both the listener and the one being listened to. Simply being offered the dedicated space in which to express our inner being is potent. When we accept this opportunity, what arises in us is often much more profound and unexpected than we could have known. You may come prepared to share your story and discover a whole different truth flowing from your mouth. You may find some very old tears to be shed, some unanticipated laughs bursting forth.

A sense of safety is pervasive in a committed circle. At its core is nonjudgment. Also at its core is respect. The cleansing and belonging fostered by this combination are magical in their capacities to nurture self-knowledge and self-acceptance. Great healing takes place, and with it comes an extraordinary and delicate kind of blossoming.

Fifty-Two Weeks of Material

Week 1

Inquiry: Beginning the Journey

For our first inquiry, let us consider our own process of *moving toward that which we desire*. Over the next several days, allow yourself to consider the following questions, being mindful of what resonates for you:

- What is your dream? What song vibrates in your heart of hearts?

- Look to identify what you would like to change … practice being specific, perhaps admitting to yourself something you have long denied. To be able to reach for something new, we must open our hands and release what they have been holding onto. What might you be holding onto beyond its usefulness? Sorting the dross from the gold is intrinsic to this process.

- Become conscious of claiming your own personal time and don't hesitate to use it for yourself. Time is a form of treasure, and you are worthy of that treasure. The ability to value yourself is a direct link to the source of your power.

This week, we will also select a name for our circle. A circle's name carries the intentions of that circle's journey, as individuals and as a group. Come to know your own expectations for our circle, the needs you hope to fill, the opportunities you anticipate exploring.

1

Linda Laws

Meditation: Casting the First Circle

Visualize yourself sitting in our circle of beautiful women; lay your hands at your sides, relaxed and open, next to the hands of the women you visualize sitting on either side of you. Allow your feet to relax and stretch out fully in front of you, toes extended forward, almost touching the circle of feet that blooms like a small starburst in the center of our larger circle.

Gently inhale and exhale deeply, three times. As you exhale, let go of the day, allowing any stresses you may be carrying, any thoughts or concerns you may have, to simply fade away as you watch them disappear into the evening light.

Continue a deep and rhythmic breathing. Relax the top of your head, relax your forehead, and allow your third eye to slowly open. (Pause.) Using your etheric eye, gaze softly upon the women sitting with you. Feel the warmth, the common bonds of womanhood. Begin making contact with each woman around the circle in silent greeting … "Hello my friend, my sister" … one by one … until you have connected with each of the women in our group. … Exhale slowly and allow your energy to sink deeply into the planet as it steadfastly rotates beneath you.

We ask for the presence of Mother Earth this evening for our gathering. We ask for clarity, light, and perception.

We respectfully call in the four directions and the four elements as they are variously known in the many Native American traditions:

We ask for the presence of the energies of the west and the element of water as we gather ourselves for introspection, cleansing, and release. Shift your awareness to the empty space behind your eyes as it reveals the black and infinite pool of your unconscious.

We ask for the presence of the energies of the north and the element of earth with their celebration of knowledge and strength, patience, and wisdom. Finding yourself enveloped in a rosy-red glow, relax in the embrace of Mother Earth.

We ask for the presence of the energies of the east and the element of air, bringing with them the forces of protection, clarity, renewal, and the spirit of spring; allow yourself to see our circle bathed in a golden yellow light.

And finally, we ask for the presence of the energies of the south and the element of fire as we embrace our fertility and transformation and prepare to dream ourselves into our visions. Notice a brilliant white light entering into your body and illuminating it from within.

Become conscious of the energies of the four directions and the four elements surrounding you, casting their protective powers around the entire circle. Allow yourself to see with a new sense of clarity. Feel a new sense of empowerment settle into your solar plexus and become conscious of the expanded light field that now surrounds your body.

As we prepare to reunite for our gathering, silently thank the four directions and elements and begin to bring your focus back to your room, to the circle of women surrounding you, as we prepare to share our thoughts this evening about what we are intending to move toward.

Closing Quote: Boldness Has Power
(Johann Wolfgang von Goethe)

> Whatever you do or dream you can do—begin it.
> Boldness has genius and power and magic in it.[3]

---

[3] Johann Wolfgang von Goethe, public domain.

ą

Week 2

Inquiry: Potential Loss

Placing our communal feet in deeper water, let's further consider a concept presented in our last inquiry: *we must open our hands and release what they have held to reach for something new.*

It is an alluring, if somewhat activating choice of action, suggesting as it does *potential loss*. And yet this loss does not feel like a ripping away; rather, it is a gentle opening up, a voluntary release, letting in the light and creating new space. It is a matter of recognizing the right time and letting go.

It has been said that in order to move from the realm of shadow into the light of creativity, we need to *listen intently to ourselves.* And to escape our own deafening inertia, we need to let go.

In the wake of our shared intentions and dreams in our last gathering, what is it we now need to release? What closely held beliefs, what protective behaviors, what attitudes, masks, or limitations will you lay aside now in your commitment to revision yourself and your life?

Meditation: Earth Light Meditation

Inhaling and exhaling completely, breathe yourself into a place of calm and centeredness, releasing the thoughts and concerns of your day. Allow yourself to relax completely into this moment.

Now, bring your attention to the base of your spine and pause there. Breathe deeply into this space. Feel the breath enter and expand into your spine, bringing with it a fine mist of golden light that slowly begins to travel all the way up your spinal column to the top of your head, casting a golden glow throughout your body.

Now, feel the light begin to slide back down, slowly moving the whole length of your body, until it arrives again at the base of your spine, and watch as it leaves your base chakra and moves out and down, plunging deep into the earth like a current of electricity connecting your body to the very center of the planet.

Allow this cord of light to breathe, to pulsate as it connects you securely to Mother Earth. Remember to inhale and exhale, deeply and slowly, allowing the light to continue to flow down from the very top of your spine to the depths of the earth. Feel the physical pull as the light flows down, taking with it all the negative and dark energies that have been lodged and held in your chakra system, carrying them out of your body and down into the earth. Relax, breathing easily and smoothly, and allow yourself to let it all go. (Pause.)

And now become aware that the light is returning to you. … Feel the current move slowly and powerfully up from the earth and back into your root chakra, a channel of clear, brilliant light slowly making its way up your spinal column, illuminating each of your chakra centers in turn as it finally reaches to the top of your head and flows out your crown into the night, like a fountain of shimmering, golden light.

Allow yourself to bathe in the light cascading over your body, leaning your head back, feeling it fall on your face, your hair, your shoulders, rejuvenating your skin as it flows down and all around you and, finally, back into the earth. Allow the light to continue falling on you for as long as it will.

Be still, breathing softly, and feel the balancing, the recalibration. Thank the earth light. Thank yourself. Slowing your breath, begin to bring yourself back to your own room, your own time, and open your eyes. Welcome back.

Closing Quote: Actualizing Our Vision
(from Sue Patton Thoele, *A Woman's Book of Spirit*)

> No matter what our life has been to this point, it
> is never too late to be who we are meant to be.

Each of us arrives in this life with special talents, aptitudes, and dreams, which we add to, augment, and refine as we mature. These aspirations and yearnings are the visions of our souls, the blueprints of our very being. It is our sacred assignment to actualize our personal visions as best we can, both for our own fulfillment, and as gifts to the planet and humankind. If we sacrifice our dreams or denigrate our gifts out of fear or as a concession to others' desires, we set ourselves up for a life of disappointment and resentment.

Living our own life does not make us selfish and self-centered. Quite the contrary. When we actualize our vision, we become centered in our hearts and connected to our spirits, which naturally makes us more loving and less selfish. What are your special gifts and talents? Do you feel comfortable about how you are expressing them? What one small step can you take today or tomorrow to move towards actualizing your unique vision?[4]

---

[4] Reproduced with permission from Sue Patton Thoele, *A Woman's Book of Spirit* (Berkeley, CA: Conari Press, 2006).

Week 3

Inquiry: Allowing

The meaning of *allow*: "to give the necessary time or opportunity for."

In these times of consciousness tending, the technique of focusing on the end result and pushing through can frequently dominate our attempt to facilitate shifts in our psyche. The result can often be a *partial* sense of having arrived at our desired destination, or even a *false* sense of success.

In any process of self-change, the presence of unconscious or subconscious issues will likely be lurking, often within the very areas we ourselves instinctively tend to avoid. These core issues demand respect. They move in their own time; they reveal themselves in their own way and cannot be rushed or forced.

To fully do our work, we need to *allow* ourselves to become familiar with these issues in our hearts and bodies, feeling and sensing into them, giving them space to transform and assist us in our evolution. These facets of our process take the time they do. To declare our status as resolved or healed, without actually opening our process to these core issues, is its own form of delusion.

Allowing the course of true healing requires us to honor the time and the pathways that we must take to retrieve and integrate all the parts of ourselves, honoring the oneness.

For our inquiry this week, let's consider these ideas in light of our own revisioning processes.

Linda Laws

Meditation: A Connectedness Meditation
(inspired by "The Anonymous String: A Meditation on Connectedness," 11/26/2000 by parish minister Richard Gilbert)

Relax wherever you are, and take three deep breaths, exhaling completely, releasing the tensions of the day. Close your eyes and feel yourself sink deep into the Earth below … into the soil and down past the rocks, among the tree roots, into the darkness … and there in a cavern, a shadow form sits in front of a huge floor loom. Looking closely you see it is Spider Woman, rhythmically throwing her shuttle across the colorful warp on her loom. With each toss of the shuttle, as one thread crosses over and under another, a luminous star appears, each one tied to every other one in the web … before your eyes a billowing fabric is being created … infinite in length, sparkling and shining like real jewels, beacons suspended in the night—its beauty takes your breath away …

As you gaze at this tapestry of stars, you watch Spider Woman move to one of the brightest stars in the web, and you see the star happens to have some planets circling around it. One of those planets shines brighter than the others and is covered with lovely blue green oceans and silver-white mists like clouds of cotton candy. Quickly Spider Woman sets up her loom, right on that one bright planet, and begins to weave again. This time, whenever one thread crossed another, a living thing appears.

For what seems like a very long time, you watch Spider Woman continue to weave her new tapestry. She wove roses and pansies and daffodils into this world, she wove fruit trees and great redwoods, cactus and ponderosas. She wove all manner of birds and fish and insects. She wove moose and mountain lions, lizards and buffalo and all of the animals into her web. And every one of these living things was connected to every other thing in her weaving, and it was very beautiful.

And Spider Woman looked, and saw she was still not finished! There was something missing from the great web … so she started to weave yet a third time. This time the crossing threads created human beings—women and men and children of all colors. And each human being that she wove into her Great Web was connected to every other living thing—to all the animals, the other planets, the trees and flowers, to the mountains, the seas and the deserts, even to the distant stars. And Spider Woman looked at her web again, and she was pleased. This was the pinnacle of her heart's creation!

All of a sudden, Spider Woman slowly looks up and sees you watching her across the vastness … and she smiles that smile of hers … she recognizes you as one of her own. She reaches across her loom and gives the Great Web of fabric a gentle tug … and you feel a flutter in your chest as your heart strings vibrate in response. Perfect harmony.

You suddenly see this interconnectedness of things lives not only in myths, it also dwells in our bodies and in our hearts … it governs our science and our music, and it reaches to the stars and the greatest galaxies. We all are a part of the oneness of the Great Fabric of Existence … and Spider Woman is still weaving! [5]

Feeling a tremendous sense of belonging and joy, you prepare to leave the cavern and begin to rise to the surface again. Reemerging, you notice that when you look with soft eyes, you can just barely see the shimmering threads of web that run between you and all that surrounds you. … And following one particularly luminous thread, you find yourself suddenly back in the center of a circle of brilliant women, and you take your place among them. Welcome back.

Closing Quote: A Guest House
(Rumi)

> This being human is a guest house. Every morning is a new arrival. A joy, a depression, a meanness, some momentary awareness comes as an unexpected visitor. Welcome and entertain them all. Treat each guest honorably. The dark thought, the shame, the malice, meet them at the door laughing, and invite them in. Be grateful for whoever comes, because each has been sent as a guide from beyond. [6]

---

[5] Reproduced with permission from parish minister Richard Gilbert, inspired by "The Anonymous String: A Meditation on Connectedness," 11/26/2000.

[6] Rumi, public domain.

Week 4

Inquiry: Choice

> Two roads diverged in a wood, and I—
> I took the one less traveled by,
> And that has made all the difference.
>
> —Robert Frost, "The Road Not Taken"

This week, let us each share a story of how, in the course of our lives, we have come to a fork in the road. Despite all odds, we chose the path that was least familiar to us—a choice not encouraged by our families, or maybe not in alignment with our own histories—a choice that turned out to be just right. Or perhaps not.

Meditation: A Magenta Cleanup

Visualize a large and luminous ball of magenta-colored light floating in the room in front of you. Feel yourself begin to merge with the deep and resonant magenta hue and become aware of the harmony and balance it brings, the sense of well-being and unconditional love. Allow them to become your foundation.

From this place of well-being, gently begin to inhale the light, breathing it into your body, drawing the vibrant color into your lungs from which it flows freely throughout your entire body, down your legs to the ends of your toes, and up your back and neck to the crown of your head. Feel the light moving in spirals, looping itself endlessly throughout your body, collecting within it any troublesome thoughts, any unfinished projects, any issues you may have carried with you into the evening … allowing the light to absorb them all, keeping your body relaxed, breathing easily. (Pause.) Now envision the light moving back in from the extremities of your body, slowly making its way back toward your heart, drawing itself together once again into a cohesive ball, carrying within it all of the debris of your day.

Drawing your breath up from your heart chakra, slowly begin to exhale a long, drawn-out channel of air, gently blowing the magenta-colored ball of light out through your mouth. Continue inhaling and exhaling several times, allowing your breath to empty your body of the magenta light, releasing with it all the heaviness, darkness, or negativity it absorbed from your body. (Pause.)

When you sense you are clean, adjust your breathing and allow your own natural breath to return. Now, gently begin your process of reentry into this space and time, where you find yourself sitting in the circle with your sisters. Welcome back.

Ahh, here we all are, cleaned up and ready to consider this evening's topic.

Closing Quote: The Road Not Taken
(Robert Frost, 1920)

> Two roads diverged in a yellow wood,
> And sorry I could not travel both
> And be one traveler, long I stood
> And looked down one as far as I could
> To where it bent in the undergrowth;
>
> Then took the other, as just as fair,
> And having perhaps the better claim
> Because it was grassy and wanted wear,
> Though as for that the passing there
> Had worn them really about the same,
>
> And both that morning equally lay
> In leaves no step had trodden black.
> Oh, I kept the first for another day!
> Yet knowing how way leads on to way
> I doubted if I should ever come back.

I shall be telling this with a sigh
Somewhere ages and ages hence:
Two roads diverged in a wood, and I—
I took the one less traveled by,
And that has made all the difference. [7]

---

[7] Robert Frost, "The Road Not Taken," public domain.

ᘒ

Week 5

Inquiry: Resistance

> Like a magnetized needle, Resistance unfailingly points
> to that which we most need or want to do. The more
> important the calling or action is to our soul's evolution,
> the more Resistance we will feel towards pursuing it.[8]

—*The War of Art* by Steven Pressfield

Resistance's allies are anger, shame, and fear. Can they also be seen as *our* allies in disguise, acting as they do as an invitation to uncover our most essential selves?

This week, let's consider how these powerful opponents intrude on us as well as beckon us into our lives. As the Dalai Lama has said, "The enemy is a very good teacher."

Meditation: Bathing with the Dark Side

Imagine you are walking in an ancient Celtic land, enjoying the deep greens of the thickly forested hills, serenaded by birdsong. Your skin is warm in the sun, and you begin to feel a bit drowsy. Suddenly you are aware that you have passed through a wrinkle in the fabric of time. The atmosphere turns dense, and although not dark, there is a thick feel to the air, a coolness and a sense of something hidden. You feel unseen eyes watching as you continue along the pathway unfolding in front of you. The farther you go, the more the forest starts to feel cloying, pressing in on you from

---

[8] Steven Pressfield, *The War of Art, Break Through the Blocks and Win Your Inner Creative Battles* (New York, NY: Black Irish Books, 2002).

all sides. The trees seem strangely alive as if they too are watching, and you can hear small, furtive rustlings in the underbrush.

To your great relief, you suddenly find yourself entering an open, misty glade. Thick clouds of steam rise up from a small pool nestled in the center of a circle of massive stones. Cautiously, you sit down on the edge of the pool and gratefully lower your legs into the dark, steamy water. Beneath the surface, you feel great jets of heat rushing past your feet from some subterranean thermal reservoir deep within the earth. The water feels silken and smooth on your skin, a golden sheen shimmering lightly above its murky surface.

Closing your eyes, you allow yourself to be drawn into the pool, until even your head is submerged under the golden-green water. Strangely, you find you have no difficulty breathing under the water. Rather, as you inhale, you feel a euphoric energy circulating throughout your entire body. This energy travels into every small space of your being, leaving in its wake a peaceful feeling of equilibrium and purity. Open your heart to this new sense of balance.

Floating, submerged, in your new, clean state, you open your eyes and allow them to gaze around you, down into the depths of the water. And there, lying at the bottom of the pool, you see a dark, formless shape. Although you cannot see any eyes, you again sense you are being watched closely, as it rests motionless in the wet stillness, waiting. Calmly, you wait too … feeling into this place of darkness, continuing to gaze with soft eyes, until realization slowly dawns … that this dark form is one of your own discarded emotions … an abandoned thoughtform. Moving closer, you can feel the power of this emotion drifting in the waters around you like a current, touching you with its rawness … its acute sense of being outcast.

Instinctively, you reach out your hand and allow the euphoric energy to flow like a transmission into the heart of the darkness. And as you watch, the inky patches begin to leach slowly into the water, eventually dissolving completely. In their place, there is now a beautiful, translucent light that merges into you without a trace. Relax into this process of transmutation. Continue circulating the light energy, breathing yourself to a place of completion. You feel a great sense of peace now, with the reclamation of this part of yourself that you have not understood or known how to accommodate or hold.

14

As you begin to sense it is time to return, visualize your body rising slowly from the depths of the pool, back up to the surface. And as your face emerges again into the billowing steam, take a few deep breaths into your lungs, exhaling out any feelings of grief or loss. Allow yourself to embrace a renewed sense of wholeness.

Lit from within, you happily make your way back through the fold in the fabric of time. And resuming your easy walk through the green, rolling hills, you come soon enough to a group of sisters sitting in a circle. Come, sit with us. Share.

Closing Quote: Give Us What You've Got
(inspired from a passage from *The War of Art, Break Through the Blocks and Win Your Inner Creative Battles*, Steven Pressfield, 2002)

Are you a born writer? Were you put on earth to be a painter, a healer, a teacher, an apostle of peace? In the end, the question can only be answered by action. Do it or don't do it.

It may help to think of it this way. If you were meant to cure cancer or write a symphony or replenish the ozone, and you don't do it, you not only hurt yourself, even destroy yourself, you hurt your children, you hurt me, you hurt the planet.

You shame the angels who watch over you and you spite the Almighty, who created you-and-only-you with your unique gifts for the sole purpose of nudging the human race one millimeter further along its path back to the Divine.

Creative work is not a selfish act or a bid for attention on the part of the creator. It's a gift to the world and every being in it. Don't cheat us of your contribution. Give us what you've got! [9]

---

[9] Steven Pressfield, *The War of Art, Break Through the Blocks and Win Your Inner Creative Battles* (New York, NY: Black Irish Books, 2002).

Week 6

Inquiry: New Eyes

Valentin Louis Georges Eugene Marcel Proust, a man of deep wisdom, has widely been considered to be one of the greatest authors of all time—definitely a kindred spirit to we edge dwellers, as evidenced by his words:

> If a little dreaming is dangerous, the cure for it is not to dream less, but to dream more, to dream all the time!

> The voyage of discovery is not in seeking new landscapes, but in having new eyes.[10]

Having been captured by the allure of Marcel Proust, this week's inquiry is taken from his thoughts on the voyage of discovery. This week, share with us how the concept of *new eyes* might augment your own voyage of self-discovery.

Meditation: Becoming One with a Tree

Relax and take three deep, sweet breaths. Allow your breathing to become soft and slow. In your mind's eye, see the trees that live in your favorite forest. Think of them as they are in the early spring, before the buds begin making their way onto the tips of their branches, stark, naked, and beautiful in the early-morning light. As you gaze at the trees in your forest, notice one tree in particular seems to beckon you, inviting you to join it. In your mind's eye, glide over to that tree and allow yourself to enter into its trunk, to become one with its woody and rooted self. Feel the

---

[10] Marcel Proust quotes, public domain.

calmness inside the tree. Savor the quiet, the inner sense of peace, the timelessness, the stability.

Breathe deeply, inhaling the essence of the tree, noticing any smells or any colors that may appear to you. As you inhale and exhale, allow your breath to travel down your body to the earth and into the roots of the tree. Allow your awareness to follow the tree roots, down, deep into the soil and the gravel, past the rocks and pockets of water, into the darkness that extends to the very center of the planet.

Remain still, inhaling and exhaling, deepening this connection with the earth through your own roots, which now intermingle with the roots of the tree, reaching down into the darkness. With each breath, draw in the energy that emanates up to you from the earth, circulating it throughout your whole body and blowing it out again, allowing all tightness, all stress, any dis-ease or toxic thoughts to be exhaled along with it.

As you empty yourself of all negative thoughts and toxins, realize how light and buoyant you feel, how free and easy your breath comes and goes. Notice you can begin to feel a tingling in the ends of your fingers, as your own limbs start to wake up. And as you feel this life force growing inside you, you also notice the new life awakening inside the tree, a flow of vibrant energy making its way up from its roots into the branches, carrying within it the tree's intention of rebirth. Feel the connection between you and the tree; allow the earth to infuse you both with healing energy, creativity, and renewed life.

Take a few gentle breaths and make a note to remember how this rootedness feels, how resourcing the earth is for you, how essential the connection with nature is for your essence. This is the place of spiritual spring.

In your mind's eye, begin to prepare for your return to ordinary time and space, slowly moving back out of the tree and into your own body. As you become comfortable once again in your human form, remember to thank the tree and to thank the earth for welcoming you. Taking several deep breaths, allow yourself to feel grounded and centered. Open your eyes. Welcome back.

Closing Quote: Thinking Outside the Box
(Lawrence Anthony)

> I have never understood the saying 'to think outside the box.' Why would anyone sit inside of a box and then think outside of it. Rather, just get out of the box.[11]

---

[11] Lawrence Anthony quote from Goodreads.com, founder of Thula Thula Private Game Reserve, Zululand, South Africa.

Closing Quote: Thinking Outside the Box
(Lawrence Anthony)

Week 7

Inquiry: Pretend It!

> Time and Space is where you chase things you pretend
> you *don't* have ~ love, friends, and abundance ~ while
> worrying about things you pretend you *do* have ~
> problems, challenges, and issues. Until one day, you
> happen to notice the prophetic powers of pretending.
> Pretend it! Thoughts become things …
> choose the good ones![12]
>
> —Mike Dooley, © www.tut.com

Have there been times when you have seriously journaled or
prayed or envisioned something and—lo!—it became a reality?
Share one of your favorite stories with us as we meet again in the
ever-loving void …

Meditation: Star Chakras Meditation

Close your eyes. Imagine with all your senses what it would feel
like if you were naked in the light of the full moon, moonbeams
cascading down upon you, enveloping your body in a mantle of
silver light. Breathe deeply, filling your lungs with the moonlit
evening, cool and shimmering … then exhaling slowly, gently.
Feel all the worries, stresses, and tensions release from your body,
from your mind, from your heart, and allow yourself to slowly
turn inward. Relax in the arms of the moon. Invite her sacred
feminine energy to nourish your own feminine nature. Feel

---

[12] Reproduced with permission from Mike Dooley, *The Universe Talks,*
© www.tut.com.

her lunar energies caressing your face and blessing your body. Experience her divine feminine presence.

Take your awareness now to the top of your head and imagine a perfect lotus flower nestled in your seventh chakra, your crown chakra, pearly white with pink tips, rotating ever so slowly. Notice the blossom is slowly growing larger, expanding its radiant petals out into the heavens beyond your crown chakra and far into the universe. Sense your crown chakra opening fully and feel the feminine energies of the moon begin flooding into your whole being through your open crown.

Now, move your awareness to a space about six to twelve inches above your crown chakra to an energy center called the soul star chakra. The soul star is your eighth chakra. It is your personal connection to universal consciousness, to your higher self, and to your soul's purpose. Some say your soul star chakra connects you to past lives. Imagine another divine lotus blossom, this one a delicate golden hue. Observe this glorious blossom in your soul star chakra as it slowly rotates, spiraling around and up, extending its luscious petals deep into the universe. Feel your soul star chakra open fully as a tremendous inpouring of light and divine energy flow into your soul star chakra and then down to your crown and throughout your whole being, bringing perfect balance to your soul star chakra.

And now bring your awareness to the soles of your feet and to the earth star chakra, which is located about eight to twelve inches below your feet. Located outside of your etheric body, this is your ninth chakra and connects you to the earth, to the nature kingdom, and to the oneness of all life. Relax as you feel your own etheric roots leave the base of your spine and move down into the space beneath you to intertwine with your earth star chakra. Savor the sense of grounding and connection this brings. Remember to breathe. Become aware of the burnt sienna colored lotus blossom resting within your earth star chakra, the tips of its petals pointing downward toward the earth, slowly spinning and expanding itself down toward the center of the planet. Allow the earth star chakra to pull the earth's energies up into your feet, bringing an increased sense of foundation, vitality, clarity, and intuition.

Once again, be mindful of the divinely feminine presence of the moon as she holds you gently in her liquid silver embrace. Breathe in her light and her love; allow yourself to be healed.

Sense the calm in your system as the light energy is channeled through your crown chakra, your soul star chakra and your earth star chakra. Ask that you receive exactly the right amount of star chakra energy that your system is capable of assimilating at this time in your evolutionary journey. As you prepare to leave, remember to thank the moon, the earth, and the nature kingdom for their many gifts. Begin to make your way back to the evening and to the circle of moon-kissed beings you now find sitting with you as you carefully settle into your physical form. Continue breathing deeply for a moment to quiet yourself. Open your eyes. Welcome back.

Bring your focus now to our topic for the evening: thoughts become things!

Closing Quote: Fantasy
(Carl Gustav Jung)

> Without this playing with fantasy, no creative work has ever yet come to birth. The debt we owe to the play of the imagination is incalculable.[13]

---

[13] Carl Gustav Jung quote, public domain.

Week 8

Inquiry: On the Lighter Side ... A Bee Story
(Rob Jaeger)

One morning the Happy Little Busy Bee woke up in her hive home, yawned and stretched, and smiled. Her little bee husband was already awake, drinking a little, tiny thimble of honey and reading his favorite newspaper, *The Pollen Times*. They had a little bee kiss and she got herself a small thimble of honey too. Pretty soon the Happy Busy Bee was ready to get to work. She blew her husband a kiss and flew away from her home and into the beautiful big forest where they lived.

It was springtime and the Happy Busy Bee found many colorful flowers just opening; she was so happily busy, she even forgot to eat lunch. She just went bzzz, bzzz, bzzz, all day long.

Quite late in the afternoon the Happy Busy Bee was busily working in a beautiful pink and yellow flower when a friend of hers, another Happy Little Busy Bee, flew up next to her and sat on the edge of a leaf watching her work. Suddenly her friend asked, "I wonder sometimes why we all work so much?" They stopped and looked at each other. Both of them had puzzled, but still friendly expressions on their little bee faces. Finally the Happy Busy Bee said "Well, we know all the flowers *need us* to live their lives to the fullest, to be the very best they can be! Also, *we like our work*, and we *love* the flowers! AND we make honey that everyone loves!" Suddenly a big grin spread across her friend's face, and she said "You are right, my good friend! I'm so glad you helped me remember!"

Each of them took a little, tiny sip of pollen from the blossoms they were in, and then they both jumped out of their flowers, waved to each other and bzzz, bzzz, bzzz flew away to their hive homes. That night they had another thimble of honey, talked with their families and then fell into a deep bee sleepzzzzzzzzzzz. The End. [14]

Here's the inquiry. After reading and assimilating this story, was there any part of it that stirred something inside you? Do you consciously maintain the boundaries of service to others and self? In the wild dance of your life, do you have the discernment to recognize when you are out of balance? How busy do you keep yourself? How do you rationalize it?

We all look forward to hearing whatever this little tale evokes in you.

Meditation: "Bhramari" ~ The Bee or Humming Breath Exercise
(as taught by Dr. Vasant Lad)

The humming of the bee is what opens the flower and coaxes it to release its nectar. Without the humming vibrations, the flower does not complete its full cycle.

This exercise opens the human heart and connects the heart with the throat and the crown chakra. In doing it, our "honey" is released! This exercise opens the synaptic spaces and connects all your neural transmitters which may cause you to feel tingling sensation.

---

[14] Reproduced with permission from Robert Jaeger.

To start, read through the steps completely before beginning the exercise.

To position your hands:

Hold your arms up horizontally slightly above your shoulders, elbows bent, hands open with thumbs up … your hands should be in front of your eyes.

Place your middle fingers directly below your eyebrows in the curve above your eyes, close to the top of your nose. Place your ring fingers in the tear ducts of your eyes against the ridge of your nose. And place your pinky fingers on your nose, in the indentations above where your nostrils meet your cheeks. Now, lay both index fingers on the area of your third eye. You may need to raise your elbows to achieve this placement. Then, place your thumbs on the flaps of your ears and push the flaps closed.

With your hands in place, close your mouth, separate your teeth, they should not be touching. Place the tip of your tongue against the back of your front teeth. Tuck in your chin and *inhale deeply* into your lungs. Then, extending your breath as long as you can, exhale out creating a humming sound the whole time.

Repeat this seven times, inhaling deeply, and then humming while exhaling. You may do this up to 17 times, after which you will take off! [15]

Closing Quote: The Soul Languishes
(Mahatma Gandhi)

The Soul languishes when we give all our thought to the worldly body. The main purpose of human life is to live rightly, think rightly, act rightly. Service which is rendered without joy helps neither the servant, nor the served. But all other

---

[15] Dr. Vasant Lad, Bhramari breath exercise.

pleasures and possessions pale into nothingness before service which is rendered in a true spirit of joy.

I have worshipped woman as the living embodiment of the spirit and joy of service and sacrifice.[16]

---

[16] Mahatma Gandhi quotes, public domain.

❧

Week 9

Inquiry: Female Archetypes

Just as women may be unaware of the powerful influences of the culture in which they live, they may also be unconscious of the powerful forces *within themselves* that influence what they do and how they feel. These powerful inner patterns, or archetypes, are responsible for major differences among women, as well as major differences within the life span of an individual woman.

In her seminal book, *Goddesses in Everywoman*, Jean Shinoda Bolen introduces the archetypal influences as the goddess. There may be several goddesses shaping our behavior and influencing our emotions at any one time; as we shift and evolve, so too our goddess archetypes change.

When we become aware which archetypes are the dominant forces within us, we acquire self-knowledge about the strength of certain instincts, about our priorities and abilities, about the possibilities of finding personal meaning through choices not immediately self-evident or that may even be disparaged.

The natural completion of one archetype brings us to that place of rest between where we have been and where we are going and prepares us for the next step on our pathway to embracing a new archetypal pattern.

There are myriad goddesses, but most fall within several main archetypal groups. Below are some examples:

> Athena—Goddess of power and wisdom, the warrioress, her father's daughter.

Artemis—Goddess of nature, animals, the athlete, the huntress.

Hera—Goddess of partnership, union of masculine and feminine, relationships.

Persephone—Goddess of the underworld, spirit world, occult, death.

Aphrodite—Goddess of love, sexuality, beauty, art.

Demeter—Goddess of fertility, corn mother, harvest.

Hestia—Goddess of the home, inner centeredness, solitude, community of like-minded sisters.

If you haven't already thought about your life in terms of these archetypes, consider how it may offer you new perspective about where you are now in your journey.

Meditation: Embracing the Feminine

Relax your body. Quiet your mind. Breathe slowly and deeply, allowing yourself to ascend high above the earth. See yourself moving deep into the cosmos, safely attached to the earth by a slender, golden cord. Allow your body to float weightless in space, relishing the sense of balance and harmony suffusing your energy fields.

Gradually, you become aware of a gold and pink light, shimmering in the ethers. And as you watch, the light slowly coalesces into the form of a female being. You are surprised how comfortable you feel with her, how easily you fall into her presence, and suddenly realize she represents a divine aspect of your own soul. ... You sense you have much to remember together.

Moving into the light that now radiates around you, your chakras begin to open, spinning effortlessly, filling with light and love. Your body tingles with an electric humming, and exquisite colors swirl playfully around you as you are drawn into a vortex, spiraling higher and higher, ultimately merging into a ray of brilliant light. You feel yourself pulsating with the oneness of all that is. Your consciousness expands into all ten directions as you glimpse infinity.

As the sacred feminine embraces your whole being, you also feel the awakening of a multitude of feminine aspects within yourself ~ the rebirth of music, healing, creativity, compassion, and unconditional love. You sense the awakening of your inner guide, the exuberance of your natural child within. As you float in the light, you can hear the steady background beat of your heart as it pumps with new purpose and vision. You can feel the energies of your heart and mind come into balanced alignment with your soul as you move toward your next evolutionary step. And you slip into a deep sense of peace.

As a circle of sisters acting in unison, let us take a few minutes to channel these energies out into the cosmos, enveloping the globe with sacred feminine energy, sharing this energy with all the women, men, and children who inhabit the planet. Know that by embracing the energies of the sacred feminine, and by living in accordance with your own divinity, you assist in awakening that vibration within all souls, like the chords of the piano awaken the strings of the harp.

As you prepare to move back toward the earth, remember to bring the light and a sense of expanded consciousness with you. These are the mainstays of your journey as a light worker. Following the golden cord, slowly return to your physical body, and when you are ready, open your eyes.

Closing Quote: Remember Who We Are
(an excerpt from a poem by Melissa Myers ©2012 from *We'Moon 2014*)

> And so we learn to breathe into the turbulent
> waters of our emotions
> To find the inner anchor that holds still as the
> winds of change and uncertainty
> blow through our minds, our homes, our world.
> Nowhere left to run
> Right here, Right now, Open, Ready,
> It is time to return to Wholeness
> To Remember Who We Are.[17]

---

[17] Reproduced with permission from Melissa Myers, excerpt from poem "Remember Who We Are" ©2012, from *We'Moon Datebook Calendar 2014* (Wolf Creek, OR: Mother Tongue Ink, 2014).

Week 10

Inquiry: Shadow Side of Resiliency

This week, a topic appropriate to a circle of extraordinary women, all of whom have lived their lives pushing the proverbial envelope: the shadow side of resiliency.

Working for a cause, doing our work, accomplishing our mission … exactly the position we are striving to attain, right? And yet when our lives become a marathon, even in service to our own sacred purpose, we must begin to ask, What kind of violence am I inflicting upon myself?

Much as travelers on a jet are seldom aware of the speed at which they catapult through the sky until they hit a patch of turbulence (Julia Cameron, *The Artist's Way*), so too those who drive themselves hard do not realize the degree of their push until they hit a wall. This may manifest as an accident, illness, depression, breakdown, defeat …

Share with us what you have learned about the seduction of overdrive. If we were to create a healing, energetic soup for women who don't know how or when to truly practice self-care, what ingredients would you prescribe?

Bring your soup spoons.

Meditation: Spirit Guides Meditation

Relax into your special space this evening, breathing evenly, in and out, allowing the day to be released until you are in that warm space of deep let go. Begin to draw subtle energy up your spine to your crown chakra. Exhaling, spiral the energy back down around your auric field until it reaches the root chakra, pooling at the base of your spine like a reservoir. Repeat this several times. (Pause.)

Imagine before you a golden altar standing by itself in an open space, cloaked in deep stillness and shrouded in a blue-black darkness as far as the eye can see. Candles flicker as they cast their light into the shadows, and the sweet smell of incense permeates the air, very exotic and intoxicating. Gradually, you become aware of the presence of three shadowed shapes in front of the altar. As you gaze on them, their shapes come slowly into focus, and you realize these beings are familiar to you. Almost in answer to your unspoken query, they rise, and in unison, they turn toward you ... and you recognize three of your spirit guides. Who are they? How have they guided you in the past? (Pause.)

You are surprised, as you have never seen all three together before, and it causes you to pause, watching intently as in the wavering candlelight the three figures begin to drift toward one another until all three have merged and become as one. The air suddenly seems charged with a powerful current, frequencies that vibrate outward in waves, enveloping you in a rush of healing energy. And you surrender, allowing each pulse beat to penetrate deep into your being—resuscitating you, recharging you to your core. As the divine energy continues to pour, you find yourself feeling young again, radiant and alive! Open yourself to this awakening.

Eventually, you begin to sense your vision drawing to a close. As you watch, your spirit guides gradually take individual shape and drift back into the shadows of the altar again, which has itself started to grow dim and fade. Soon it all has slipped back into the world of spirit, and you find yourself sitting in a swirl of subtle energy, pooled at the base of your spine. Use this energy to assist you to settle back into your physical body, and when you are ready, slowly open your eyes. ... Welcome back.

Closing Quote: Slave Driving Inner Mean Girls
(Christine Arylo)

Five Signs you are pushing yourself too hard:

1. *You feel crabby.* Crabbiness is a sign that your soul is starving for play and pleasure.

2. *You forget all you have accomplished and only see what you have not yet done.* You get more done in a day than most people, yet you rarely feel a real sense of accomplishment (for more than a few minutes anyway). You are always on to the next chore, the next achievement, so there's no time for rest or celebration.

3. *You put your self-care on hold.* You want to go to that yoga class, eat healthier, get to bed earlier, but it never happens. You keep telling yourself that you will eat better, go to the gym, get more sleep when you are not so busy … but you're always busy.

4. *You cancel plans because you are too busy.* Busy with work, with kids or with whatever project has currently got you embroiled; you cancel plans that would have been fun, you show up late, or you often have to say "No, I can't, I'm too busy."

5. *You sleep with your electronics …* <u>when</u> *you sleep.* You have a hard time "turning it off" … your mind, your phone, your email.

Living this way is not "normal" … it's unsustainable and unhealthy. Sure, there may be moments one needs to rally and push to the finish line; but pushing and working extra hard should be the exception instead of the norm. *CHOOSE TO PAUSE.* We can release the super-person cape, refuse to live by the unsustainable, pressure cooker pace, and pause just long enough to check in with our inner wisdom to find a different, more supportive way to operate.

The truth is, we have to be willing to "do" our lives differently, willing to say "Enough, I've done enough … no more." Then instead of feeling guilty, feel good that we've made a choice for our own self sustainability, a choice to achieve our goals, but not at the cost of our own happiness and health. When we give enough, instead of giving in excess, everyone is happier and better off.

The Four "R" steps to wiser choices:

Step #1: <u>Reflect</u>. Admit you are pushing yourself too hard. Get honest with yourself and say out loud "I am pushing myself too hard." Saying the words out loud shatters the pressure and creates space for new insight.

Step #2: <u>Re-assess</u>. Reconfigure your expectations. Close your eyes, take a breath, put your hand on your heart. Ask your inner wisdom, "What would ENOUGH look like?"

Step #3: <u>Re-Align</u>. Give yourself permission to "*just do enough.*" Take whatever actions you need to *release the excess* and *embrace "just doing enough, no more, no less."*

Step#4: <u>Remember</u>. The idea here is to create a new way to live our lives sustainably. Next time it comes to accepting a new commitment, put it through the test. Do I REALLY WANT, NEED, DESIRE to do this with all my heart? Then make a solid commitment to do or not to do it, and don't look back. [18]

---

[18] Reproduced with permission from Christine Arylo, "Slave Driving Inner Mean Girls".

Week 11

Inquiry: Unexpected Gifts

Lovely ladies of the light, have you ever received an inspired realization, a lost or missing piece? Have you been given a timely warning from nature—an animal, a rock, a tree, a storm? Have you ever been struck by the coincidental perfection of a passing bumper sticker?

Information can be received from surprising sources! This week, let's share our stories of memorable messages received.

Also this week, plan to meet in person or on the phone with one other sister from the circle, and be prepared to share with us the most unexpected thing you learned about her!

Meditation: Oak Grove Meditation

Envision yourself in a large grove of oak trees. Feel the ancient strength emanating from these great, leafy beings. As you bask in this elemental tree power, feel it revivify your physical and subtle energy bodies. (Pause.)

Shafts of light pierce the green canopy above, as finely veined leaves flutter in the faint breeze, their pods of acorns suspended on tiny stems. From deep in the shadows, you suddenly become aware of movement as a beautiful lady steps forward, like an apparition from the nature kingdom. Welcome the druidess, mistress of the forest and bearer of earthly wisdom. Allow her to share her bounty with you as she places a beautiful garland of wildflowers around your neck. You find yourself intoxicated from the delicious fragrances of the blossoms and hear her lilting song of love for the planet, just barely reaching your ears, as if being sung in some other distant realm. An overwhelming sense of abundance and love surrounds you. (Pause.)

She takes your hand and pulls you deeper into the grove, to a doorway built into the gnarly roots of a gigantic oak tree, and gently shoves you through the portal. Immediately, you find yourself in a brilliant cavern, crystalline stalagmites soaring up from the floor and massive, tapered stalactites hanging down like icicles from ceiling above, as if still dripping. … You feel compelled to sit amidst the colors and light, allowing them to penetrate you, absorbing the crystalline energies. The longer you sit, the more complete you feel. This extraordinary cave with its ancient crystalline wisdom represents the source of your clarity, your strength, the authority upon which you stand—your essential self.

Take whatever time you need to absorb the power and beauty of this place. (Pause.)

Soon, you sense it is time to return to present time and space. Rising, you look down to see a single acorn lying near your foot, its scaly, leather cap holding tightly to the smooth cupule safely containing its seed, the seed of the new. Picking it up, you take it with you as a memento of this visit with the oaks, and gathering yourself, you step back through the portal.

The forest is now covered in a shimmering, golden light, and there is an atmosphere of magic, a feeling of the rightness of things. The druidess again glides across the soft earth, pulling you into a warm embrace of farewell. And murmuring your gratitude, you bid the oak grove and its hidden crystalline cavern adieu and begin making your way back to ordinary time. As you emerge, you feel the small form of the acorn nestled in your hand, a reminder that these memories are yours to keep, resources to carry with you as you continue forward in your earth walk.

Returning to your physical body, take the time to ground and center yourself … and when you are ready, open your eyes and join the circle of sisters surrounding you.

Closing Quote: But Ask Now the Beasts and They Shall Teach Thee
(excerpt from the Sutta Nipata)

Animals, our "horizontal brothers," have long been recognized as essential to our development and well-being. Direct encounter with animals, seeing them eye to eye on their own ground, evokes a sudden wonder and respect. Their vivid life brings us alive to the source that creates and sustains all beings. Without such encounters we risk losing that part of ourselves which most deeply resonates with nature ~ the heart of compassion.

If our greatest loss with the animals has been to lose touch with the reality of their existence, our second loss has been to banish them from our minds. We assume they have nothing to teach us about the predicaments of our existence. We no longer know how to listen to the wisdom of the various four-legged, six-legged, finned and winged creatures that share our life on this Earth. We forget they are our ancestors, as well as our kindred spirits. Long before we existed, they worked out the round of life in thousands of variations as though anticipating the experiments of human cultures to come.

We are members of a human family and society, but the presence of animal "others" enlarges our perception of our Selves ... beyond the city, beyond the cultures ... and opens us inward, to that ground of being where live the lizard and monkey, the fish and the bear, the bat and the dragonfly. These are our relatives. They are, like us, offspring of the great mystery and intrinsic to a balanced and living whole. [19]

---

[19] The Sutta Nipata, excerpt from "But Ask Now the Beasts and They Shall Teach Thee."

Week 12

Inquiry: Ritual

This week let us ponder *ritual*. Rituals can provide an outward manifestation of an inner change. At their root, rituals tap into the timeless archetypes of the cycles of death and rebirth. There seems to be a universal human feeling that one's natural birth is not enough; there is a desire to regularly wipe the slate clean and begin things anew, to separate and to reunite, to change form and condition, to die and to be reborn.

Share with us some of your experiences with the rituals you have used in your own process of self-discovery. Do you have a favorite ritual? Have you had uncomfortable experiences with rituals?

Meditation: Ball of Light Meditation

Relax and allow your body to completely melt into the surface on which you are reclining. Release the tension from your hands and adjust them so they lie partially open. Allow your spine to uncoil and expand. Breathe deeply by inhaling in through your nose, bringing the breath into your lungs and all the way down to your Hara. When you exhale, draw the breath up from your Hara, back through your lungs, and out your mouth. With each inhale, visualize yourself breathing in love and empowerment, and with each exhale, visualize breathing out negativity and fear. Repeat this pattern three more times, gradually slowing your breath. (Pause.) Take one final breath in through your nose, hold it for a count of five, and then exhale it completely out through your mouth. (Pause.)

Visualize your feet surrounded by a shimmering ball of golden light—beautiful, warm light so soft you can feel it caressing your skin. With the ball completely enveloping your feet, become aware of a soft, buzzy sensation that transmits a deep sense of peace and protection as you feel yourself fall together.

Now become aware of the discharge flowing out from the bottoms of your feet, a current of light carrying within it the negative energies and toxins that have been collected and held within your body. … Allow them to be drawn out now, relaxing the soles of your feet as they allow the negative energies to be channeled back to the earth to be neutralized. (Pause.)

Moving this ball of brilliant light slowly up your body, sense a heightened life force flowing within you as the light draws out the toxins and recharges your body with clean and vital cosmic energy. Allow the ball of light to expand and make its way up to your torso, saturating the center of your body with warmth, inviting your cells to relax and release. Feel the ball move down your arms into your hands, to the tips of your fingers … and then up your neck to the crown of your head. (Pause.) Surrender to the warmth, the vitality, the gentle relaxation, all the while allowing the discharge to continue its flow, carrying the negativity down and out your feet. (Pause.)

Remain in deep relaxation for another few moments, radiating this peace and contentment out into the universe. Know that you can enter this relaxed and clean state whenever you desire. In doing this ritual, you reconnect with Mother Earth and once again become one with her.

When you are ready to make the shift back to your ordinary reality, prepare to emerge from this place of deep calm, while allowing the feeling of it to remain with you. Take three slow breaths to steady and ground yourself. With each breath, feel yourself become more fully refreshed and aware of the pure energy surrounding your body, inside and out. Exhaling, slowly open your eyes to reorient to your room again. Welcome back!

This evening, our inquiry asks us to ponder the use of ritual in our lives.

Linda Laws

Closing Quote: A Purification
(Wendell Berry)

At the start of every spring, I open a trench in
the ground.
I put into it the winter's accumulation of paper,
Pages I do not want to read again … useless words,
fragments, errors.
And I put into it the contents of the outhouse:
light of the sun, growth of the ground, finished
with one of their journeys.

To the sky, to the wind, then, and to the faithful
trees, I confess my sins:
That I have not been happy enough, considering
my good luck;
Have listened to too much noise;
Have been inattentive to wonders;
Have lusted after praise.

And then upon the gathered refuse of the mind
and body, I close the trench,
folding shut again the dark, the deathless Earth.
Beneath that seal, the old escapes into the new. [20]

[20] Reproduced with permission from Counterpoint Press, Wendell Berry,
"A Purification" from *New Collected Poems* (Berkeley, CA: Counterpoint
Press, 2012).

Week 13

Inquiry: The Challenge of the Nodes

Many of you are familiar with astrology's nodes of the moon. If not, check out Jan Spiller's book *Astrology for the Soul,* or Elizabeth Spring's *North Node Astrology: Rediscovering Your Life Direction and Soul Purpose.*

The tug of war between your north node (toward which you are moving) and your south node (from which you are disengaging) can be illusive, confusing, and tricky to navigate. Behaviors that have served you well for the first part of your life may no longer bring successful results as you move toward early midlife. And yet your new repertoire, the skills, aptitudes, and attitudes of the north node that are your lessons to master, may seem risky, unreliable, and unfamiliar.

Frequently, when attempting to make a decision that activates the changing of the guard from the south to the north node, you may find yourself in an impasse while remaining unaware of its true nature.

Typical elements of a struggle of the nodes may look like this:

- You find yourself in a challenging situation.

- The situation seems to demand seemingly dichotomous choices be made.

- The choices are perplexing and seriously challenge your (professed) stability and comfort zone.

- You wonder, *Can I do nothing and simply maintain the status quo?*

- But you sense movement through the issue is *requisite for growth at a soul level.*

- You are confused about which choice is which!

- You feel activated and passionate about the dilemma and, though exhausted, cannot simply let it go.

- The really bothersome thing is that the situation feels like an iteration of an old pattern.

Share with us how you are negotiating these waters between your old need-to-move-beyond south node behaviors and risking the move into the unknowns of your north node destiny. If you need to refresh yourself, read up on your north node!

Meditation: The Pearl of Truth

Breathe yourself into a relaxed state. Visualize yourself in a warm mist on a mountaintop. See before you a small orb floating before your eyes. It is opalescent and reflects the colors of the rainbow, like a beautiful pearl. As you rest your eyes on the pearl, watch as it begins to move toward you, very slowly, expanding until it has become large enough to envelop your whole body … and it does. Inside the pearl, it is warm and softly lit, and you feel an overwhelming sense of coming home. As you rest refreshed and protected, you realize this is the inner sanctuary of your deepest knowing, the source of your inner voice. This is the home of your own personal truth, and you begin to listen deeply.

As you listen, you are suddenly certain that this is the answer to all that you have been searching for your whole life; you realize that if you can only hear this truth, there will be nothing more for you to find. It is a revolutionary concept: your personal truth lives and breathes within you! Whatever you are doing, it is your truth. It is truth's footsteps walking along your path, meandering, making their way through the physical world. You are sleeping; it is truth softly breathing in and out, journeying to other dimensions. You are speaking; it is truth murmuring, singing, teaching, laughing.

You are silent; it is truth that is hushed, waiting, alive in the dark potential of no noise.

And you settle. You resolve to live your truth … vibrant, radiant, blessed. Your whole life becomes an ode to the truth you carry, your gift to yourself, your contribution to our world.

As you begin to stir, filled with these visions, you notice that the air around you is shifting as your pearl is now transforming back into a small glowing orb, floating, dancing in front of your eyes. You notice it now hangs connected to a golden chain that you take in your hand and fasten around your neck. Feel the pearl orb lying gently in the hollow of your throat, radiating its steady and reassuring presence. Returning to the present, know that this portal into your inner truth sanctum is available to you whenever you wish.

Slowly breathe in and out three more times, shifting your awareness back to the room where you find yourself sitting among eight other women in a circle of light. See the pearls hanging delicately around each of their necks, radiant and beautiful. Bringing yourself fully back, prepare to share your gratitude, breakthroughs, and thoughts on this week's inquiry—old patterns as looked at through the shifting of the nodes.

Closing Quote: Waiting with Truth
(inspired by an excerpt from Shannon L. Alder)

> Not long ago, I learned that if I let other people tell me how Spirit was supposed to work in my life, I would be dead. If I would have given in to someone else's version of God, that I would have done nothing to improve my situation. The notion that "if it was meant to be, it will be," is a pacifying yet potentially harmful quote that many spiritualists use to soften the blow of anger and disappointment. The Universe is not passive. It is relentless and will build you through fire. It will put in your heart a need for answers. The intensity of what bothers your soul is often the voice of the Divine trying to take you from a limited vision of humankind to the full-on view

of the best life available to you. Inner peace is only found through action. Fear may darken the trail, but the light of peace stands at the end of such a journey—waiting with truth. [21]

---

[21] Shannon L. Alder, "Waiting with Truth," excerpt from Goodreads.com.

Week 14

Inquiry: Persons of Influence

Often, we find there are one or more persons of major influence in our lives, people who act as our guides, teachers, and friends. They can be allies in the forging of our soul lessons or may be the agents of change as we are forced to grow in order to master our greatest challenges. They may appear briefly or stay for a lifetime.

Who do you find in your life that fits this category? What resources has this person provided for you? How has their influence altered the trajectory of your life? How do you understand who *you* are to *them*?

Meditation: For a Person of Major Influence Now Passing Over

This evening, I would like to begin our call by casting our circle and quieting our minds. Relax your bodies, close your eyes, and allow all tension to drain away from you. Relax the space between your eyes and enter into the darkness you find just behind your forehead in that area of the third eye. Go as deep into that darkness as you can. You may find colors there in the darkness—allow them to breathe with you.

From this place, let's extend our etheric hands outward from our bodies to clasp the outstretched hand of the women next to you … until we have closed the ranks of our circle. … And now looking around, see all of us standing in our radiance, beautiful sisters of the light. Notice the circle has begun to rotate to the left, slowly, and our feet are beginning to move to a rhythm not heard with our earthly ears …

Let us consciously bless this space. … Feel the energy of the circle intensify and deepen in its glow as we all continue the large, slow, turning … like a graceful dance. Feel the warmth and depth of this delicious energy on your skin. Allow it to soak into your being.

Now, still clasping the etheric hands of the sister on either side of you, bring your arms up above your head until you can see, in your mind's eye, a circle of hands raised high above the turning circle of women … and see a fountain of light rising up from the ground beneath the dancing feet. Watch as it moves through our hearts, up our arms and out through our hands, collecting itself into a powerful beam of multicolored light that shines out into the deepest heavens.

Ask that this light travel to that place and space of in-between where the mortal being called "(insert a name)" now makes her way to the unknown—across the boundaries between life on earth and life after death—her final journey for this lifetime. Ask that she be bathed in this sacred light as a last embrace from Mother Earth and from we who still remain on the planet. Ask too that her family be wrapped in the warmth and glow of this light now being gifted to "(insert name)" by our circle. Let us intend and attend to this sacred crossing, each in our own way.

If there are others you would like to offer this light to, please include them here now. (Pause.)

When you feel complete, allow your arms to return to your side. Thank the earth for her infinite flow of light and for the use of it this evening. Allow your own natural breath to return. Slowly open your eyes. Welcome back.

And now let us speak of our own experiences of friends, guides, angels, and other emissaries sent from the beyond to assist us in our personal earth walk.

Closing Quote: Angels and Other Supreme Beings
(Sue Patton Thoele from *A Woman's Book of Spirit*)

Our spirit wants to surrender to that which it perceives as higher and holier than itself. We need noble role models and a god is hard to visualize. To resolve this dilemma, and yet not singe our circuits to a frazzle with Her overwhelming power and majesty, I think the Beloved encourages angels and other emissaries to intercede on Her behalf. A widely held belief affirms that at least two angels are entrusted with our care at birth, and that others, including the Archangels themselves, are happy to assist us when we call upon them.

I have never seen an angelic being with my physical eyes, but I know several very down-to-earth people who have. On several occasions, however, I have been lovingly protected and guided by invisible, but obviously present, forces. I like to think that these forces were angels, celestial beings of some kind, or energy from my own higher Self. Given my experience, and others I've heard about, I can't help but believe that just outside our range of perception we are encircled by angels and guides, the spirits of those whom we have loved and lost, and other emissaries, either from our personal soul selves or in the guise of other humans, who befriend us. And with that certainty comes incredible peace of mind.[22]

---

[22] Reproduced with permission from Sue Patton Thoele, *A Woman's Book of Spirit* (Berkeley, CA: Conari Press, 2006).

Week 15

Inquiry: The Light of Summer Solstice

As a kiss to the sun, the planets, and the stars, this week we honor the summer solstice. The longest day of the year, summer solstice is a time of powerful energy and radiant light.

Let us bring the solstice light into our circle this week and use it to provide clarity, forgiveness, and resolution.

What might you have been keeping in the dark that would now benefit from being brought out into the light for acknowledgment, examination, and transcendence? How might you be unencumbered by doing this?

Meditation: A Gift of Love
(inspired by an excerpt from Mike Dooley from *The Top Ten Things Dead People Want to Tell You*)

Take a few deep breaths and relax as I tell you a story …

> Everything is sacred;
> Thoughts become things;
> Love is all … always there, everywhere, needing
> no approval, no judgment, bearing gifts that do
> not need to be earned or deserved;
> Love is Light.
>
> Consider, if you will, this love as just described,
> as a translucent, iridescent light, cascading upon
> you from above, all around you, arriving in
> unrelenting waves. Imagine it bathing you like

sunshine, drenching you like rain, caressing you like air, and illuminating everything. So enveloping that you can even breathe it into your lungs.

This love pierces you with its utter simplicity, energizes you, lifts your spirits, makes you smile unceasingly as you bask in its overwhelming ecstasy. This love IS, as much as you ARE.

Imagine too that as you observe the physical world around you, which suddenly seems to be as translucent as the light of love illuminating it, you realize all things are OF this love. It's not that the love shines ON the objects of time, space and matter, but that these things ARE it … just as white caps on the tips of the ocean swells, pushed by the wind, are part of the very ocean they roll over. You see that this love, in its flowing, can take form, intelligently follow patterns, can organize itself with purpose and intention. Then a new revelation hits you, and in total awe you consider that if everything around you is love, dancing apparitions that can see one another, this must mean YOU are exactly the same as what you are seeing. YOU are a part of this dance, a dancer yourself. You see you truly are of the Divine, a falling raindrop among countless others, a God[dess] self-reflecting within time and space.

You are a part of the plan, and yet also now a Plan Maker, as you choose new directions to aim your awareness.

You rediscover what is so obvious – all is exactly as it should be. There is no other agenda. Nothing else has to happen … *you are love.* This is the gift of awareness that you give to yourself. The Gift of the Light." [23]

---

[23] Reproduced with permission of the publisher, Mike Dooley, *The Top Ten Things Dead People Want to Tell You* (Carlsbad, CA: Hay House Inc., 2014)

Relax now and gently bring yourself back to the present, allowing the glow of love to continue to emanate from you as you join the group of radiant women who sit in the light, in wait. Welcome back!

Closing Quote: True Light
(White Eagle)

> The True Light is a gentle illumination, which, rising in you, causes you to look on your world with understanding and compassion and respect. When you respect the souls of your brother and sister, you respect their lives in every way. This gentle spirit, this respect one for another, must come. For this is the generation of the One True Light. And this True Light is that of Love.[24]

---

[24] White Eagle.

Week 16

Inquiry: Alter Ego

It's shape-shifting time. Let's shed our personas. From a blank slate, choose an alter ego that you really would like to try on, something that we would not expect. Change your name, your vocation, your gender even. ... Write the script for an alternate life that you would like to live, even if only for the evening.

Meditation: Shedding the Persona
(Meditation written by a Cantonese woman from *Earth Prayers: 365 Prayers, Poems and Invocations from Around the World*)

Make yourself comfortable and breathe in and out, deeply and rhythmically. Relax the space between your eyes and allow yourself to listen to the sound of my voice. (Pause.)

> You sit down on a hilltop, or anywhere high
> enough for you
>   to see nothing but the sky in front of your
>   eyes.
> With your mind you make everything empty.
>
> There's nothing there, you say.
> And you see it like that – nothing
>   emptiness.
>   Then you say, AH,
>   but there IS something.
>   Look! There's the sea!
>   And the MOON has risen –
> full, round, white.

And you see it like that –

>Sea, silver in the
>moon light,

with little white-topped waves.
And in the
Blue Black sky above
hangs a great moon Bright,

>but not dazzling,

a soft brightness you might say.

>You stare at the moon a long,

long time, feeling calm, happy.

>then the moon gets *smaller*,

but brighter and brighter and brighter till you
see it as a

>pearl, or a seed,
>but so bright

>you can only *just bear* to look at
>it. The Pearl

starts to grow. And before you know what's
happened it's

>KUAN YIN herself, standing up against
>the sky

>all dressed in gleaming white

and with her feet resting on a lotus

>that floats in the waves.

>You see her
>once you know how to do it
>as clearly as I see you,
>Her Robes
>are shining
>and there's a halo
>round her head.

>She smiles at you

such a lovely smile. She's so glad
to see you that tears of happiness sparkle
>in her eyes.

>If you keep your mind
>calm,

by just whispering her name
and not trying too hard
she will stay a long
long time

When she does go
it's by getting smaller.
She doesn't go back to being a pearl
But just gets so small
That at last you can't see her.
Then you notice
that the sky and the sea
have vanished too.
Just Space is left.
Lovely, lovely, Space, going on forever.
That Space stays long
if you can do without *you*. Not you *and* Space,
you see.
Just Space.
No you. [25]

This is the shedding of the persona. This is clearing the way for the new.

Into this place of emptiness, I place our talking stick. Our inquiry this evening is to identify one of our many possible alter egos and share this with our sisterhood.

Closing Quote: Mindfully Listen
(E.C.R. Lorac, 1938. Edith Caroline Rivett lived 1884–1959, a British crime writer who wrote under the pseudonyms E.C.R. Lorac and Carol Carnac.)

Mindfully listen to your thoughts, they form your words;
Mindfully listen to your words, they form your actions;
Mindfully listen to your actions, they dictate your habits;
Mindfully listen to your habits, they establish your character;
Mindfully listen to your character, it reveals your destiny. [26]

---

[25] Reproduced with permission from the publisher, Meditation by a Cantonese woman, from *Earth Prayers: 365 Prayers, Poems and Invocations from Around the World,* edited by Elizabeth Roberts and Elias Amidon (New York, NY: Harper One 1991), page 386.

[26] E.C.R. Lorac quote.

Week 17

Inquiry: Dynamic Tension

Ladies of the light,

Ponder ... What is one area of your life where you have one foot on the gas and the other foot on the brake? What might you do to resolve this dynamic tension?

Or maybe there are some payoffs for remaining in gridlock?

Meditation: Blue Moon Meditation

The lunar cycle corresponds metaphorically to an evolutionary cycle, from darkness (new moon) to light (full moon), or from unmanifest to manifest. With each completion of the lunar cycle, we are given a new chance to bring about the realization and manifestation of our intentions, our goals, and our dreams.

Find a comfortable position in which your body is open to receiving the etheric, silvery gold moonlight. Sit or lie with your arms by your sides, palms facing up. Extend your feet out, toes together, gently pointing. Close your eyes and take a deep breath ... in through your nose ... out through your mouth. Repeat this several times until you feel your body relax. (Pause.)

In your mind's eye, visualize a diamond shape, each point of the diamond glowing with phosphorescent, divine light. Your head rests at the top point, your feet lay at the bottom, your hands mark the sides, and the center of the diamond lies just over your solar plexus. Feel your body ground itself, sinking your roots deep into the earth, as you slowly allow your solar plexus to open.

Visualize a channel of beautiful, silver-gold moonlight flowing directly into the center point of your diamond as it moves into and through your solar plexus. Allow it to fully illuminate and purify your solar plexus and then begin to travel throughout your whole body. Feel this cleansing and purifying light as it flows down into your root chakra, magnetizing and drawing to itself the dark and toxic energies that you are ready to release to the moon. When you feel grounded and ready, allow the light to slowly move up to your second chakra, your center of joy and creativity, collecting and taking with it all the negative energies that may be residing in your Hara. Feel the silver-gold light as it continues to make its way to your solar plexus, filling all the spaces, gently and persistently cleansing and empowering. Now feel the light move through your solar plexus and upward to purify your heart chakra. Allow yourself to feel an abiding sense of compassion, love and profound truth as your heart is filled with silver-gold moonlight. Next, allow the light to enter and fully illuminate your throat chakra, removing all blocks and stagnant energies. Feel the freedom and clear intention in your throat chakra. When you are ready, release the light to journey up even farther into your third eye, completely filling your ajna with beautiful, purifying, silver-gold moonlight. Notice the clarity and the healthy glow within your third eye, as if illumined from within. (Pause.) And finally … see the moon's energy flow into your crown chakra, bringing with it a deep sense of calm, peace and connection, and then coursing up and out the top of your crown and back into the night.

Notice the rays of light weaving themselves around your body in a beautiful matrix pattern, connecting you with the greater universe. See yourself bathed in the clean, clear, shimmering silver-gold moonlight. Sense the light that still resides in each of your chakras as it continues to attract and collect the dark and stagnant energy that you are now releasing to the moon. Feel this light presence begin to stabilize your energetic bodies and allow it to expand and grow stronger.

When you are ready, slowly bring your awareness back to the room where your body reclines and open your eyes. See the moonlight still around you on the etheric plane. Know that when you fall asleep tonight, the peaceful lunar energy will continue working its healing within your body and will stay with you over the next several days.

I am now placing the talking stick into the soft, golden moonlight at the center of our circle.

Our inquiry this evening asks, In what area of your life do you sense resistance or an immunity to impending or desired change, a feeling of accelerating and braking at the same time? What might you do to break that dynamic tension, or are you deriving benefit at some level from remaining in this highly charged state?

Closing Quote: You Are Not on Earth to Make Things Happen
(Mike Dooley from tut.com)

> You are not on earth to make things happen. You are not on earth to spread the love. You are not on earth to make it a better place or to learn acceptance of the things you cannot change. You are not on earth to find your soul mate or your purpose. You are not on earth to put the needs of others before your own. And you are most certainly not on earth to suffer, pay penance, be tested, or judged.
>
> Did I leave anything out?
>
> You are on earth because in your loftiest state of being, perched high above the wonderment, at the pinnacle of your glory, you wondered what it would be like, even fleetingly, to believe in limits.
>
> You sage,
> The Universe
>
> And when you can grasp this, from within the illusions, you will also grasp how unlimited you truly are. (And we'll probably never hear the end of it.)[27]

---

[27] Reproduced with permission of Mike Dooley, *The Universe Talks*, June 9, 2015, © www.tut.com.

Week 18

Inquiry: Spiritual Bypass

Spiritual bypass is a consequence of kidding ourselves about the true origin or nature of our attitudes and behaviors *in the name of spiritual attainment*. Subtle and often insidious, our posturing and delusions may be difficult for us to admit or even to recognize.

Check out the list below with an eye toward detecting your own possible spiritual bypassing:

- Do you use spirituality to escape from reality or to avoid dealing with a fearful or painful situation?

- Have you allowed yourself to be taken advantage of or abused in some way, in the name of compassion, or karmic destiny?

- Have you ever overlooked an obvious red flag in a situation or in a personal relationship, because you allowed yourself to become enamored with the spiritual story?

- Do you couch your own shadow behaviors in spiritual terminology?

- Have you censored emotional responses such as fear and anger, or feelings of exclusion or envy, dismissing them as negative and unenlightened emotions?

- Have you ever justified or rationalized otherwise inappropriate behaviors based on your presumed or perceived spiritual evolvement?

These traps are not for the spiritual teachers or practitioners alone. They lurk in the unexamined shadows of all of us.

This week, let's shed some light on this tendency. By doing so, we can evoke greater wakefulness, authenticity, and kindness toward ourselves and others.

Meditation: A Bubble Meditation

Let's enter into our time together this evening by breathing gently and deeply, inhaling and exhaling in balance. Lean back in your chair, recline on your bed or pillow. … Wherever you are, adjust your body until you feel completely and utterly comfortable. Relax and close your eyes.

Visualize bubbles rising up around you, lots of pastel-colored, shiny bubbles, opalescent, rising slowly up from the surface on which you are resting. See how they make their own way, up and up, each floating into the space over your head and then out the top of your room into the sky above. Become aware of the fluttering air currents around you as more and more bubbles push their way upward, brushing against your skin, cool and soft, kissing you as they pass.

Notice one bubble in particular that seems to be hovering directly in front of your face—not moving, simply floating—as if it is waiting for you. And notice that it is slowly expanding. Watch as the surface of the bubble stretches easily, becoming larger and larger. See the rainbow colors swirling on the surface, shiny, delicate …

Watching, mesmerized with the colors, you now see behind the shiny surface into a vast chamber, and you can make out faces, a bit unclear but strangely familiar. You hear merriment, peals of laughter coming from the spaciousness inside the bubble. It feels very light and inviting, like a favorite place you have known from some other time or place …

Allow yourself to slowly move toward the surface of the colors, passing through the thin, shiny skin of the bubble and into the huge space beyond the veil, filled with colors the likes of which you have never seen. The air is sweetly scented. In the far distance, you sense a group of beautiful souls seated together in what seems to be a dome-shaped room. The atmosphere is very festive, very welcoming, and feels safe and familiar to you.

You realize this is the place where your sisters meet. You can see them off in the distance and now realize they are motioning to you, calling you to join them. As you move deeper into the room, you notice a talking stick leaning up against a large crystal in the center of the circle. Taking your place among the women, you suddenly realize you have much to share with them, and you look forward to taking up the talking stick when it is your time. Silently, you wait for someone to begin …

Closing Quote: Shadowing
(Clarissa Pinkola Estes, excerpts from Women Who Run with the Wolves, chapter 15)

> The things that have been lost to women for centuries can be found again by following the shadows they cast. These lost and stolen treasures still cast shadows across our night dreams and in our imaginal daydreams.
>
> It is from that land that we step into our day clothes, our day lives. We travel to that wildish place in order to sit before the computer, in front of the cook pot, before the window, in front of the teacher, the book, the customer. We breathe the wild into our corporate work, our business creations, our decisions, our art, the work of our hands and hearts …
>
> The wild feminine is not only sustainable in all worlds, it sustains all worlds.
>
> Women dream the same dreams worldwide … We are never without the map. We are never without each other. We unite through our dreams. [28]

---

[28] Clarissa Pinkola Estes, excerpts from *Women Who Run with the Wolves* (New York, NY: Penguin Random House, 1992), chapter 15.

Week 19

Inquiry: The Point of No Return

Drifting along in the currents of life with a choice to be made—distracted, dithering, weighing the pros and cons of the matter, perhaps avoiding or denying—and suddenly, or gradually, you become aware of having *passed the metaphorical line beyond which there is no turning back*. The die is cast, and you must continue the course forward.

Whether it is a principle of physics or psychology, or derives from some mystical dynamic, crossing the metaphorical Rubicon can be quite compelling.

What might be the benefits or challenges of reaching the point of no return? How has this experience swept you into the next evolutionary step on your pathway? In hindsight, what was the interplay between your conscious and unconscious intent?

Until then …

Meditation: A Dance of Creation

As we enter into the evening hours, gently lay your body down, sitting or reclining; it makes no difference. Get comfortable and allow the weight of the day to drift away from you. … See it go in streaks and greasy smears … flowing out of your body and up and away into the ethers to be transmuted. Watch it all go and relax into your clean state. … Enjoy the lightness, the purity, and breathe deeply into each cell, replenishing, nourishing, cleansing, and soothing. Just sit and be still.

Close your eyes, and allow yourself to drift … (Pause.)

You are again on a mountaintop. It is humid and warm, and there is a very gentle breeze caressing your skin. Feel the wind kissing your shoulders, your neck, your hair. … The breeze makes a sweet humming sound, like an ocean far away … and you drift even further away into the currents tugging at you, etheric hands reaching for you from the wind, pulling you into a swirl of color and sound—beautiful really—exquisite colors intermingled with musical tones and chords, all rhythmically intertwining in a dance … and you feel yourself drifting into the movement, drawn as if by a magnet toward the colors and the harmonies. And soon you are swirling around and around, your body fading into a translucent state, somehow expanded, larger and more spacious, as you allow the colors and the music to penetrate you, to move through you … all of which seems intricately choreographed by some unseen power.

You feel perfectly at home, whirling and turning in the currents, following the flow. … You have been here before. It is familiar and comforting, moving effortlessly with the spirit of the light and sound in a sacred dance of creation … (Pause.)

You wonder, *Could this really be how it actually is in ordinary life?* Perhaps normally you just don't notice the patterns or the harmonics, or maybe you don't surrender to their pull. If this is so, you suddenly realize you can recreate this reality any time you wish—a place to recharge and reconnect, to realign with your own life's design, to dance your own dance, to weave your own pattern. This realization brings you a sense of happiness, safety, and you feel as if you now have a powerful ally.

Completely relaxed, you begin to sense into your body again, resting on the mountaintop. The wind is quiet now. You can hear the music fading and see the colors begin to slip away as you become more and more aware of your physical body … until you are again reclining in your room. Gently begin moving your fingers and your toes, slowly bringing yourself back to this dimension. You realize you are surrounded by potent sister energy, and you feel the reassuring presence of the women around you. This evening, we share our thoughts about this week's inquiry, *the point of no return*. Let us begin now by speaking of our breakthroughs and gratitude.

Closing Quote: What Motivates Change
(Caroline Myss)

What motivates you to change your life—I mean really change something and not just talk about changing something. Most often it takes a collision with something or someone or with a situation that forces you to shift the course you are on. Though we frequently—very frequently—receive intuitive rumblings that we need to make wiser or more reflective choices about something, we rarely pause to actually take the time to reflect on those inner rumblings, to allow for "intuitive revelation" to make itself known. That is somewhat of a slow inner and contemplative process that collides with the nature of our times, which is our passion to have everything known and done and decided in the "immediate here and now." In my humble—and perhaps not-so-humble opinion—our impatience with taking the time to make decisions through doing inner reflection leads to decisions we either make in haste or regret. And regrets make us want to blame someone. And so the cycle goes.

St Benedict schooled his monks and priests in such wisdom. He said that a person should take all the time he needed to come to a decision. Read all that you needed to read for inspiration. Speak to your Spiritual Director as much as you need. Pray for guidance. And then make your decision. Then live your decision fully, without question. Do not look back. Only move forward, for it is in the questioning of your decision and in the looking back that you initiate profound suffering. [29]

---

[29] Reproduced with permission from Caroline Myss, "What Motivates You to Change," from *Caroline's Blog* July 2015.

Week 20

Inquiry: Scarcity

Scarcity of money should never be confused with scarcity of energy.

It is said that money is a neutral substance that flows into and out of our lives, taking its direction from our intentions regarding it. It is those intentions that alter the neutral energy of money. And our intentions are primarily derived from our cultural, religious, and family-held values and rules about money.

Often, we allow money to substitute for life force energy, frequently with negative consequences. As a result, every dollar we spend can become an unconscious expenditure of our life force energy. In this instance, money *does* translate into a scarcity of energy, literally.

Our challenge is to achieve a relationship with money separate from our life force. The more impersonal our relationship with money is, the more likely we are to direct its energy appropriately in our life.

An organic and healthy relationship to money aligns with natural abundance:

- View money as simply another kind of energy that flows into and out of your life.

- Maintain a relationship with money that is free from guilt, shame, fear.

- Operate from the viewpoint that the more you create, the more there is for everyone.

- Get past the outdated notion that money is evil, or one must be poor to be spiritual.

- Recognize that by creating wealth, many other dimensions become available to you.

These healthy beliefs and perceptions must become deeply rooted at the core of our energy system. When they are, natural abundance can be manifested, not only in the spiritual realm, but on the physical, material level as well.

What blocks the natural flow of abundance into your life? By results, how successful have you been in your quest to create a bountiful life? Do you believe you are entitled to one?

Into the thicket we leap!

Meditation: The Lammas

Lammas is the cross-quarter day between the summer solstice and the autumnal equinox. It is the beginning of the harvest, which commences in late summer. Lammas has two main themes—the celebration of abundance and the waning of the light.

Taking a few deep breaths, allow yourself to sink into a place of deep peace and silence. Feel a gentle breeze fluttering softly about your head, wisps of your hair moving like the golden tassels on stalks of corn … and breathe in the warm, earthy air.

It is early evening. Feel the heartbeat of summer, the depth of it warming the land … and also the sense that summer has begun already to recede, a chill just on the other side of the heat. The days are becoming shorter as the sunrise and sunset move closer and closer together. Tall grasses whisper and murmur as they wave in the breeze, their seed pods hanging ripe and golden.

Allow yourself to feel an upswelling of gratitude for the bounty and abundance in your life symbolized by the Lammas … the plentiful harvests of vegetables and fruits, sweet and juicy, bearing shades of red, orange, and gold like the sun itself, embodying the richness of life.

As you make your way through seemingly endless fields of gold, you notice a still, quiet pond of water off in the distance, beckoning you with its wet coolness, a cloud of warm mist rising into the evening air. It is shrouded by forests of still-green leaves and drenched in evening birdsong. Suddenly, you sense the presence of several beings walking close to the water's edge, and you realize you are seeing through the veil into the etheric plane. It is soft and gauzy, an oasis of pastel beauty nestled within the summer night. You recognize the forms of what appear to be three goddesses walking hand in hand, their gowns billowing about their feet, faces silhouetted in a glow of supernatural light. In the presence of these otherworldly beings, you feel empowered and expanded, infused with silent wonderment. Their beauty is breathtaking; their essences saturate the spaces around them like an aura. In this atmosphere of grace and abundance, you feel filled to capacity, whole.

Desiring now to return to your ordinary consciousness, you turn to go back … and lying at your feet is a golden sheaf of wheat fastened with a grape vine. You take the sheaf into your arms, knowing that wheat symbolizes love, charity, and abundance. Gratefully, you make a promise to meditate on this gift from the goddesses at some future time.

Holding the wheat sheaf in your arms and your promise in your heart, step back through the veil now, into your ordinary reality. Realign yourself in your physical body, and when you are ready, open your eyes. Welcome back.

Closing Quote: Financial Abundance
(Abraham-Hicks)

> Financial Abundance does not occur in one's life because of hard work or good luck or favoritism. Financial Abundance is simply the Universe's response to consistent thoughts and feelings of abundance.
>
> There is a Life Stream that flows to you. There is a stream of clarity, a stream of wellness, a

stream of abundance—and in any moment you are allowing it or not. What someone else does with the stream or not, does not have anything to do with how much of it will be left for you. You are never deprived when someone else gains, because abundance expands proportionately to match desires. When the success of another makes your heart sing, your resistance is gone and your own success soars. This stream is as abundant as your ideas allow it to be.

Make peace with outrageous abundance. You are more likely to have a pure vibration and attract more abundance if you leave money out of the equation. But it isn't because money is the "root of all evil." It's because your beliefs about money usually have a tendency to mess up your vibration.[30]

---

[30] Reproduced with permission from Abraham-Hicks, "Financial Abundance," excerpt from *Abraham-Hicks* online, ©Jerry and Esther Hicks, AbrahamHicks.com (830)755-2299.

Week 21

Inquiry: Myths as Themes for Our Lives

And now to stir the fantastical …

Clarissa Pinkola Estes teaches that within every woman there is a wild and natural creature, a powerful force filled with good instincts, passionate creativity, and ageless knowing.

In an effort to reconnect with that self, we often attract into our lives a story, a tale or myth through which we breathe vitality back into our truest natures.

What myth or myths do you recognize as the leading themes in your life?

Meditation: Grandmothers' Meditation
(Holadia)

> Sink back into the space you have provided for yourself this evening. Notice all of the little ways you can get comfortable, making adjustments, breathing expansively into the myriad of dusty inner corners of your body. Again, take a deep breath.
>
> Allow your mind to let you begin to travel, placing your feet upon the path that appears through those tall trees to your left. Follow it around the bend as the warm, gentle air caresses your body in movement, making your way through the bird song, out past the tumble of rocks to the earthy

fragrance of the flowered meadow, rich with lupine.

There the Grandmothers are gathered to rest and enjoy one another's presence. Become aware of the deep stillness and quiet, the softness and touch of coolness to the air and the delicious fragrance of the earth beneath you.

The Grandmothers have gathered to share their wisdom about honoring our true nature, which they impart telepathically and kinesthetically in silence this evening. Sink into that wavelength and listen gently—rest. Notice the contact your body has with the Earth—your feet, your tush, your back, your head. Allow your body to receive the wild and natural truths offered by the Grandmothers. Notice what bits of wisdom are blossoming in your heart or mind. Receive it. Welcome it. Breathe into it. Soften and rest. Let the stillness sink deeply into you, easing your bodymind.

Quietly offer thanks and prepare to leave the Grandmothers' circle. Rising slowly, follow the path out of the meadow, through the tall trees, back to your own space. Carry the wisdom received with you, in you, maintaining that sense of presence and peace.

Arrive back fully into the space you have created for yourself for this evening's call. Sink in again, getting comfortable. Tonight we've come together to share our gratitudes and breakthroughs, and to explore the ancient stories and myths that shape our lives as women. [31]

---

[31] Reproduced with permission from Holadia.

Closing Quote: Fairy Tales, Stories, and Myths
(Clarissa Pinkola Estes excerpts from *Women Who Run with the Wolves*, introduction)

Fairy tales, stories, myths provide understandings which sharpen our sight so that we can pick out and pick up the path left by our wildish nature. The instruction found in story reassures us that the path has not run out, but is still there, leading us deeper and more deeply still, into our own knowing. The tracks we all are following are those of the wild and innate instinctual self.

I call her Wild Woman. When women hear those very words, wild and woman, an old, old memory is stirred and brought back to life. The memory is of our absolute, undeniable and irrevocable kinship with the wild feminine, a relationship which may have become ghostly from neglect, buried by over-domestication, outlawed by the surrounding culture, or no longer understood anymore.

Once women have lost her and then found her again, they will contend to keep her for good. Once they have regained her, they will fight and fight hard to keep her, for with her their creative lives blossom; their relationships gain meaning and depth and health; their cycles of sexuality, creativity, work and play are reestablished; they are no longer marks for the predations of others; they are entitled equally under the laws of nature to grow and to thrive.

Wild Woman is the health of all women. Without her, women's psychology makes no sense. [32]

---

[32] Clarissa Pinkola Estes excerpts from *Women Who Run with the Wolves* (New York, NY: Penguin Random House, 1992), introduction.

Week 22

Inquiry: Living Our Gifts

Night Talk's David Viscot has been quoted as saying the following:

> The purpose of life is to discover your gift.
> The work of life is to develop it.
> The meaning of life is to give your gift away.[33]

All of us are born with inherent gifts, talents, aptitudes, and skills. Not only can these innate aspects of ourselves be elusive, they can be both our biggest challenges and our most profound blessings.

For this week's koan, let us share what we have discovered in the process of living our own gifts.

Meditation: Sending Out Prayers

This evening, let's place our bodies in a comfortable position, whatever feels just right, and relax fully into the falling light of the evening. Allow your breathing to calm and choosing a color, or more than one color, begin breathing that color into your lungs, allowing the breath to circulate slowly throughout your chest. And then move the color into the rest of your body. Allow it first to move up into your throat and to the space behind your eyes, continuing upward to the top of your head … even visualizing it rising above your head to cleanse the space above your crown chakra. Then slowly allow the color to flow back down to your shoulders and out your hands to the ends of your fingers. Allow the light to loosen any constrictions and to remove any blockages. Breathe it now into your heart area,

---

[33] David Viscot quote.

circulating it around and then down, deep into your abdomen, gently massaging and cleansing. Continue breathing the colors in. Allow the light to move down the length of each leg to the ends of your toes … and then watch as it moves out from your heels, flowing into the ground beneath your body. Continue breathing slowly and deeply, allowing the colors to move wherever they are drawn, always and finally out the bottoms of your feet. (Pause.)

You may feel tingly as the light sweeps your body clean. Allow the colors to illuminate every crevice of your body and feel the release of each cell as it expands and breathes, maybe for the first time in a long time. (Pause.)

From this state of grace, let us send pure and radiant energy to the planet. Bring your etheric hands up and visualize light flowing from them, beautiful golden light, moving as a current out from the palms of your hands. Send this channel of light wherever you are drawn to send it, to any who may benefit. In your mind's eye, see a stream of healing light carrying blessings and love to the darkest corners of the universe and into the coldest hearts. See the forests become lush and green, the sky become clear and blue. See human faces soften and become peaceful and healed. See the plant kingdom, the animal kingdom, whole cities bathed in light, as the light continues to pour from your body, out through your hands like a powerful electromagnetic current flowing through you. Surrender to this experience for as long as it continues. (Pause.)

As you drift back toward your regular state of awareness, allow yourself to recognize the astounding power of this light … and know that there is no difference between the recipients of the light and you. We are not simply sending light and healing *out to others*; we are also receiving it ourselves. This light you are feeling in your body is the light you are sending. On the deepest level, we are one with it all. By sharing what we have gained in our meditations, we reaffirm our harmony with all of creation.

Slowly bring your attention to your body lying still. And begin to collect the thoughts you would like to share with the sisterhood this evening. Tonight's inquiry is about both the blessings and the challenges of manifesting one's own gifts.

Closing Quote: Giving
(Osho, *The 99 Names of Nothingness*)

Love is innocent when there is no motive in it, no duty. Love knows nothing of duty. Duty is a burden, a formality. Love is a joy, a sharing; love is informal. You have too much, so you share, you want to share.

And whoever shares with you, you feel grateful to him or her, because you were like a cloud—too full of rainwater—and somebody helped you to unburden. Or you were like a flower, full of fragrance, and the wind came and unloaded you. Or you had a song to sing, and somebody listened attentively, so attentively that she allowed you space to sing it. So to whomsoever helps you to overflow in love, feel grateful.

Imbibe that spirit of sharing, let that become your very style of life: to be capable of giving without any idea of getting, without any condition attached to it, giving just out of your abundance.

And slowly the ripples start reaching farther and farther. You love first your Self … and then you love other people; then you start loving animals, birds, trees, rocks. You can fill the whole universe with your love. A single person is enough to fill the whole universe with love, just as a single pebble can fill the whole lake with ripples—a small pebble. Be a pebble. [34]

---

[34] Osho, "Giving," from *The Ninety-Nine Names of Nothingness: A Darshan Diary* (Zurich, Switzerland: Osho International Foundation, 1980).

∽

Week 23

Inquiry: Dreamed-of Gifts

Deepening, as it should be …

Beyond the gifts excavated in the course of last week's inquiry, this week, let's dig even deeper into our psyches.

What aptitudes, talents, or skills might you secretly (or not so secretly) yearn for? Is it possible that these dreamed-of gifts could be learned or developed? If so, how could that possibly be achieved? And if so, how might that change the trajectory of your life as you are currently living it?

Leaping joyously into the void again! Love your spirit!

Meditation: Ho'o Pono Pono
(Dr. Ihaleakala Hew Len, prayer) [35]

This evening, settle yourself, relax your mind, relax your body … and begin by inhaling through your nose and exhaling out through your mouth, bringing yourself to a place of complete and utter tranquility. Breathe in the peace and circulate it throughout your whole body.

Ho'o pono pono is a Hawaiian healing practice, a mantra for forgiveness and correction. It means literally "to make things right." When we feel and say the words of the Ho'o pono pono Prayer, we take responsibility for ourselves and our part in the world we create around us.

---

[35] Dr. Ihaleakala Hew Len prayer

By clearing ourselves with love, forgiveness, and gratitude, we clear the experiences of the past, the present, and the future. When we get in touch with our deepest feelings of compassion, forgiveness, and gratitude for ourselves, we experience a great healing, and we then have the capacity to love and heal others.

Words spoken with intention create vibrations that break up old patterns of fear and negativity. The words of the Ho'o pono pono Prayer, "I'm sorry, I love you, please forgive me, I thank you," are so powerful, they heal the collective as well as the individual. They open the heart and allow love to flow.

You may wish to make your Ho'o pono pono chant into a kind of song. Song is the language of the heart. Singing, chanting, laughing, and crying all release stagnant energy and emotions and break up old patterns that no longer serve us, moving the old energy up and out.

For the next few minutes, let's repeat the Ho'o pono pono Prayer as a chant, until it becomes almost as a mantra. In your mind's eye, begin by envisioning someone or something, some event you would like to release—you may find more appearing as you go through this process—allow them to come. Hold that person, that thing, or that event now in your heart, and begin chanting the Ho'o pono pono Prayer, either to yourself or out loud …

> "I'm sorry,
> I love you,
> Please forgive me,
> I thank you …"

(Pause for chanting … two minutes.)

It is said, that when chanting Ho'o pono pono, *we* are being breathed by the Breath of Spirit and sung by the Song of Life.

Gently, let's begin to make our way back to this side of the field and reorient to our physical bodies, to our rooms, our candles, to our circle … bringing the focus now to our inquiry for this evening, which asks us, what are our secretly desired gifts, skills, aptitudes, talents? Is it possible to achieve them? And how might that change our lives? I now place the talking stick in the center of our circle. Who would like to start by sharing their breakthroughs and gratitude this evening?

Closing Quotes: Two Reed-Flute Quotes
(from Rumi)

A craftsman pulled a reed from the reedbed, cut
holes in it, and called it a human being.
Since then, it's been wailing a tender agony of
parting, never mentioning the skill that gave it
life as a flute.

God[dess] picks up the reed-flute world and
blows.
Each note is a need coming through one of us, a
passion, a longing pain.
Remember the lips where the wind-breath
originated,
and let your note be clear.
Don't try to end it.
Be your note. [36]

---

[36] Rumi quotes, public domain.

Week 24

Inquiry: Your Vessel

There is a book called *A Pearl in the Storm* written by Tori Murden McClure. It's her story of how she became the first woman ever to row solo across the Atlantic Ocean. Her twenty-three-foot boat is constructed of Kevlar and plywood and named the *American Pearl*. Tori rowed 2,961 miles in eighty-one days in the *American Pearl*. Among other life-changing lessons engendered by this woman's heroic journey was the reminder of how important it is for us to care for our vessel. Even in the middle of Hurricane Danielle, as she was being brutally hurled about her small cabin, this woman was epoxying leaks as they were being torn in the Kevlar membrane of her little boat.

This week's inquiry asks, What important vessel do you have in your life that you routinely rely upon for your well-being in the world? What infrastructure—physical, social, mental, spiritual— is vital to maintaining your health, your balance, your ability to thrive? Are you attentive to the maintenance of your vessel? Or do you find little time for its caretaking? How effective are you at knowing and balancing your priorities?

Meditation: Ajna Cleanse

Begin by drawing a deep breath in through your nose, holding it there for a moment and then exhaling it slowly back out through your nose. Repeat this several times. Allow your senses to truly feel the air moving into and out of your body. … Feel the coolness of it and listen to the gentle whisper it makes as it passes through you, in and out.

Allow yourself to see a color dancing in front of your Ajna, the chakra we also call our third eye. Choose one of your favorite colors, one that brings you tremendous joy and a feeling of well-being just looking at it. (Pause.) Gently draw that color into your third eye and allow it to completely fill the whole space, which suddenly seems even larger than you imagined. Feel how natural it is to have this beautiful color in your Ajna, like a filter through which all your thoughts and images flow.

Now, move your focus to your fifth chakra, your throat. Be receptive to whatever you find there; it may be a vision, a sound, a memory. When you can see it clearly, begin to inhale in through the color now pulsating in your third eye, bringing your breath down to your throat chakra. Allow the breath to pulsate and circulate freely throughout your throat area. When you exhale, channel your breath directly out from your throat chakra, allowing any toxins or energetic debris to flow out with it.

Next, move your attention to your heart chakra and look again to see what you have been carrying in your heart. Gently begin to inhale your breath through the color in your third eye, drawing it down and into your heart chakra. Allow the breath to move into and around all you carry in your heart, drenching it in the colored breath of your third eye, collecting whatever negative energies there may be and channeling them out as you exhale slowly and deeply from your heart chakra.

And finally, bring your attention all the way up to your crown chakra. Be open to any visions that may appear to you, holding them lightly in your conscious awareness. Listening to the sound of your own breathing, begin again to draw a deep breath in through the color in your third eye, bringing it up into the crown chakra, swirling the colored breath around and around your crown and out the top of your head like a fountain. Exhale deeply as you allow the breath to leave, taking with it the impurities and blockages collected from your crown.

In the stillness, become aware of a profound sense of balance and equilibrium now pervading your physical form. If you find any thoughts passing through your mind, observe them all and release them all into the outflowing of your breath. If you sense emotions coming to the surface, acknowledge them and allow them too to be lovingly exhaled out through your breath.

Resting and serene, slowly allow your own natural breath to return and gradually become aware of your body lying still. Gently settle back into your physical form, slowly moving your fingers and toes. When you are ready, open your eyes, bringing yourself back to the present moment, here and now. Welcome back.

This evening's inquiry asks, How well do you care for your vessel?

Closing Quote: The Path of the Hero[ine]
(adapted from Joseph Campbell, *The Hero with a Thousand Faces*)

> We have not even to risk the adventure alone, for
> the hero[ines] of all time have gone before us ...
> the labyrinth is thoroughly known. We have only
> to follow the thread of the hero path.
>
> And where we had thought to find an abomination,
> we shall find a god[dess].
> And where we had thought to slay another, we
> shall slay ourselves.
> Where we had thought to travel outward, we
> shall come to the center of our own existence.
> And where we had thought to be alone, we shall
> be one with all the universe. [37]

---

[37] Joseph Campbell, "The Path of the Hero," from *The Hero with a Thousand Faces* (Princeton, NJ: Princeton University Press, 1968).

Week 25

Inquiry: Circle as a Vessel

Women in transition, courageous women bravely stepping out: into a new home, into a mountain community, moving to a different state, becoming engaged to be married, assisting a parent to pass over, taking a maybe-permanent break from a mate, marrying off a son, terminating a longtime job, achieving new levels of competency at work. Women gifting themselves time—for solitude, for physical fitness, for rest and creativity—moving at such velocity, not fully realizing our own changes. It is normal to yearn for rest and comfort when changing so rapidly. What we learn to do is rest in motion, like lying down in a vessel under full sail.

One of our vessels is circle.

Circle propels us forward by gently clarifying our self-awareness, by promoting our self-growth, and then provides a safe haven to recuperate from our forward motion in the arms of the sisterhood—accepting, encouraging, inspiring, nurturing.

In light of last week's inquiry, consider your relationship to our circle. How attentive are you to the maintenance of this vessel? Or do you find little time for its caretaking? Again, how effective are you at recognizing and balancing your priorities?

Until then ~

Linda Laws

Meditation: Falling Together
(Osho, from "Ordinariness" from *Osho Zen Tarot: The Transcendental Game of Zen*)

Relax as I take you on a magic carpet ride of imagining.

Sometimes it happens that you become one, in some rare moment. Watch the ocean, the tremendous wildness of it—and suddenly you forget your split, your schizophrenia, you relax. Or, moving in the Himalayas, seeing the virgin snow on the Himalayan peaks, suddenly a coolness surrounds you and you need not be false because there is no other human being to be false to. You fall together. Or, listening to beautiful music, you fall together.

Whenever, in whatsoever situation, you become one, a peace, a happiness, a bliss surrounds you, arises in you. You feel fulfilled.

There is no need to wait for these moments—these moments can become your natural life. These extraordinary moments can become ordinary moments—that is the whole effort of Zen. You can live an extraordinary life in a very ordinary life: cutting wood, chopping wood, carrying water from the well, you can be tremendously at ease with yourself. Cleaning the floor, cooking food, washing the clothes, you can be perfectly at ease—because the whole question is of you doing your action totally, enjoying, delighting in it. [38]

Sit for a moment and contemplate those aspects of your life that you would like to fully occupy—those things that are so easily rushed through or done on automatic—and create an intention to ease yourself fully into those activities, those interests, those relationships, those creations.

(Long pause.)

---

[38] Osho, excerpt from "Ordinariness," from *Osho Zen Tarot: The Transcendental Game of Zen* (New York, NY: St. Martin's Press, 1994).

When you have come to a place of understanding and commitment to living your life as you would really like to live it—alive, radiant, intentional—make a promise to yourself that you will honor this commitment. Make that promise now. (Pause.)

Carefully stepping from the magic carpet, slowly bring your consciousness back to your body reclining in your room and open your eyes to find yourself surrounded by a circle of women. And when you are fully returned, prepare yourself to take up the talking stick and speak of your gratitudes and breakthroughs for this week, and to share your thoughts on this evening's inquiry about our *communal vessel* we call circle.

Closing Quote: Everything Is Done in Circles
(Black Elk)

Everything the Power of the World does is done
in a Circle.
The sky is round, and I have heard that the Earth
is round like a ball, and so are the stars.
The wind, in its greatest power, whirls.
Birds make their nests in circles, for theirs is the
same religion as ours.
The sun comes forth and goes down again in a
circle.
The moon does the same, and both are round.
Even the seasons form a great circle in their
changing, and always come
back again to where they were.
The life of a [person] is a circle from childhood
to childhood,
And so it is in everything where power moves. [39]

---

[39] Black Elk, Oglala Sioux holy man.

Week 26

Inquiry: You as Doyenne

As we move through the chronological stages of our lives, so too do we move through the psychological and spiritual aspects of ourselves as women.

Doyenne is a French word for "the oldest, most experienced, and often most respected woman in a group; a female elder."

As a doyenne, what might be the most significant lessons, life-altering realizations you have to share with the younger women in your lives? As a future, older doyenne, what guidance would you offer to your current self?

With bated breath …

Meditation: The Soul Signature

Sit quietly for a moment and breathe deeply, inhaling and exhaling. Relax your body, release your mind. Feel a sense of peaceful gratitude permeate the space in which you are. Imagine your soul self before you and invite her to enter into your heart.

Together, begin walking down the curving and moss-covered footpath that appears in the distance. The pathway is surrounded by a colorful vapor, like pastel clouds that swirl away from you as you move through them, light and airy. Allow the clouds to wash away the dust from the day as you are drawn deeper and deeper into this misty valley of light.

Eventually, you come upon what appears to be an ancient stone temple. Its door is slightly ajar, and the interior glows softly, lit from within by a multitude of glowing orbs scattered about its perimeter. Curious, you approach and cautiously step over the threshold into a hushed and hallowed salon.

Standing in the partial shadows, you suddenly realize that what had appeared to be lights are actually reflections from the surfaces of dozens of mirrors, all hanging on the walls at varying heights—large mirrors, small mirrors, oval shaped, square, irregular, round. Some of the shimmering glass surfaces are enormous, bordered by ornate molded frames; others are petite and framed by colored wood or burnished metal. Some of the mirrors are covered with veils or lie hidden under layers of cobwebs.

As you slowly walk around the room, you find yourself gazing into each silver glass until the reflections within each are transmitted back to you, crystal clear. (Pause.) Allow yourself to receive the many versions of your selves as they span the ages of your lifetimes—younger and older, joyous and sorrowful, defeated and victorious—embracing all the many aspects of your integrated self.

You have now circled the entire room. Feeling quite sated, you begin to move toward the temple door when your eyes are mysteriously drawn to one last mirror on the wall. It hangs by itself from a delicate linked chain. Its surface is cloudy, strangely obscured or obstructed. Standing directly in front of the mirror, you gaze into its opaque surface. What is it that prohibits you from seeing clearly into the depths of the silver glass? Remain open to possible intuitive messages or suggestions on how you might clear away any impediments, inhibitions, or obstacles … (Pause.)

As you contemplate the dark surface of the mirror, invite a picture or sense of who you will be at an older age to come into your heart. As you begin to see this future self, notice the mirror has lost some of its obscurity. Deep in the glass, you can begin to see the translucent details of that future self. … Allow this self to more fully embody her reflected form, witness her innate strength, behold her striking beauty, treasure her essence. *From your sacred place in her past, encourage that older self to flower into the unique and exquisite blossom she is meant to be in your future.* Know that she symbolizes your soul signature made manifest.

Take a moment to gaze one last time into the depths of this mirror, fixing the memory of its images in your heart. Filled with immense gratitude, you are ready now to leave the room and begin your journey back through the misty pastel clouds. Allow your mind to review all the many ages you have grown through—envision them all and bless them all. Give thanks for the joys they have bestowed, the sorrows weathered, and the wisdoms gathered. Bless this woman who is you, this exquisite being you can now begin to see in her entirety. And acknowledge her for her many gifts in this lifetime and for those still to come. As you return to your ordinary state of consciousness, allow yourself to gently settle into your physical form. When you are fully returned, open your eyes. Welcome back!

Closing Quote: Gather the Women
(Jean Shinoda Bolen, excerpt from *The Millionth Circle*)

> The Millionth Circle is a metaphor for the circle that, added to the rest, brings about a critical mass that ushers in a new era. Every Circle that considers themselves part of the Millionth Circle Vision is linked through their intentions. There are probably millions of people who are unknowingly affiliated in their hearts.

> Any woman can be an influence where she is. And if you are in a circle that supports what you are doing, all the better. When women gather together, they naturally share stories. They learn, they find encouragement, they discover allies and share grand ideas. Women as a gender, not every woman, but women generally, have a wisdom that is needed.

> It is time, now, to Gather the Women. [40]

---

[40] Reproduced with permission from Jean Shinoda Bolen, *The Millionth Circle* (Berkeley, CA: Conari Press, 1999).

ço

Week 27

Inquiry: Throat Chakra, the Bridge

Last week, we spoke of the guidance we would offer to the younger women in our lives from our place as elders, as doyenne, as well as the wisdom we would gift to our future selves.

In order to have guidance to offer, we must be able to hear our own inner voices. We must live in alignment with and express our truest values. The channels connecting our physical, psychological, mental, and spiritual selves must be open.

Energetically, our lower chakras represent our physical body (first chakra), emotional body (second chakra), mental body (third chakra), and relational self (heart chakra). Our third eye and crown chakra are linked to our more subtle realms of being—intuitive, occult, and spiritual.

On the energetic plane, the throat chakra bridges the lower and upper chakra systems, like our neck connects our torso and head on the physical plane. The throat chakra's element is ether, as in ethereal.

This week, let us consider our own relationship to our throat chakra.

- How integrated are you between who you are on the inside and who you are on the outside?

- Do you live your life in alignment with your spiritual values?

- Are you able to fully express yourself using all the different mediums available to you, not only verbally but also through your actions, your creativity, the totality of your being?

- What is your relationship to truth, your own truth as well as others' truths? Are you able to hear truth, recognize it, speak it, honor it?

Listening for you in the deep.

Meditation: The Bridge of Blue Light

Allow your eyes to close and feel yourself sink down into your own breath, relaxing into your physical body, softening your mental body until you can actually feel the earth holding you in her embrace, supporting you as you finally let go. Feel the weight of your physical self slip away, allowing you to lie weightless, suspended in serene silence. Notice the silver cord of light that safely connects you to the earth and relax completely.

From this place of deep rest, calmly watch your energetic body as it floats peacefully in that place between worlds. See the electric currents of color that surround each of your energy centers, the brilliant and vibrant hues of red, orange, yellow circulating effortlessly throughout your lower body … the deep, clear green flowing in and around your heart. Now see the saturated hues of indigo and violet as they rise up from your third eye and out the top of your head like a fountain of shimmering light, cascading down to be drawn up again in the great cycle of life inspiriting life.

Breathe slowly and deeply, knowing you are held safely in the arms of existence and that existence cares for you.

Now, from your place of peace, bring your attention to the space between your head and your lower body, the lovely expanse of your throat chakra. See the beautiful matrix of blue light radiating out from what appears to be an intricate network of fibers, a luminous web of light-filled strands extending from the upper region of the heart, all the way to the center of your third eye.

See the pulsating wavelengths of blue cast their intense energies into the chakra system, illuminating the channels between the spirit world and our physical world of manifestation.

Take several moments to be with your throat chakra as the spectrum of blue light weaves its way into your energy field. Notice what colors are predominant, which colors seem to be dim. Look closely at the connection between your throat and your heart and lower chakra centers. Is it clean and solid? Look too at the connection between your throat and your third eye and crown. Are they fastened securely?

Know that this bridge between your spiritual and physical energy centers is the conduit through which you communicate with your whole self. Whatever you find, hold the information gently and bring that knowledge back with you.

Begin now to close your chakras down a little, holding the intention in your mind's eye, sensing the calming of their energies. Feel the embrace and support of the earth beneath you as it slowly brings you back through the ethers to the denser realm of our ordinary reality. Hold yourself lovingly. Take an extra moment to acknowledge the uniquely beautiful being that you are. (Pause.)

When you are ready, bring your focus back to the room where you are sitting. Look around you to see the beloved women who join you this evening in the etheric gathering of this circle of light. Prepare yourself to share your gratitudes, any breakthroughs you have had this week, and speak to the inquiry of your relationship to your fifth chakra, the throat chakra, home to your self-expression, creativity, and communication. Welcome back.

Closing Quote: The Naming
(excerpts from Judith Duerk, *Circle of Stones*)

> How might your life have been different if there had been a place for you, a place for you to go to be with your mother, with your sisters and the aunts, with your grandmothers, and the great- and great-great-grandmothers, a place of women, to go, to be, to return to, as woman?

> A place where you were nurtured from an ancient flow sustaining you and steadying you as you sought to become yourself—to help you find and trust the ancient flow already there within yourself—waiting to be released …

A place where other women, somewhat older, had been affirmed before you, each in her time, affirmed, as she struggled to become more truly herself ...
A place where, after the fires were lighted, and the drumming, and
the silence, there would be a hush of expectancy filling the entire chamber ...
a knowing that each woman there was leaving old conformity to find her self ...
a sense that all of womanhood stood on a threshold.

How might your life have been different, if, long ago when you were still a tiny child you began to come to the Women's Lodge as the normal cycle of your life, you heard for the very first time what the women called the Naming ... each woman speaking slowly into the stillness, sharing her feeling of how she saw her life and what she wished to say of it ... sharing it with the women around her ... weaving the threads of her life into a fabric to be given and named.

A place where, after the fires were lighted, and the drumming, and the silence, you would claim, finally, in your Naming, as you spoke slowly into that silence, that the time had come, full circle, for you, also, to reach out ... reach out as younger women entered into that place ... reach out to help them prepare as they struck root in that same timeless earth.

How might your life be different? [41]

Go in peace, beloveds.

---

[41] Reproduced with permission from New World Library, Judith Duerk, *Circle of Stones* (Novato, CA: New World Library, www.newworldlibrary.com), ©1989 by New World Library, excerpts from the preface, and pages 32, 47, 85, 112.

Week 28

Inquiry: The Art of Sexuality

This week, let us venture into the sacred universe of sexuality. Frequently misunderstood or burdened with the weight of unresolved emotional or cultural baggage, let us consider sexuality in its purest form—as an intricate balance of life force energies, a rhythmic dance of our own masculine and feminine within, and the attunement of our deepest creative impulses and expression.

From this perspective then, consider the following:

- Is your sexual identity in alignment with your overall self-identity?

- Is your sexual behavior in alignment with the way in which you live your life?

- Do you experience your sexuality as separate and distinct from, or as an integral part of, other creative channels in your life?

- Without too much thought or censorship, write down ten words that illustrate your beliefs and feelings about sexuality.

- Consider sexuality through the lens of aging. How were you sexual as a child? How did your sexuality evolve as you moved through adolescence, early adulthood, middle age, elderhood?

- And, finally, contemplate your sexual energy as a dynamic of your chakra system, originating in your second chakra and, as your consciousness becomes more integrated, advancing up through fourth chakra (and beyond).

Come prepared to let your hair down!

Meditation: Our Integrated Selves

Settle yourself for the evening and begin breathing slowly and deeply, gently drawing your breath in from the crown of your head, allowing the breath to circulate throughout your physical form, moving it down and out through your root chakra to the earth below. Now at the same time, begin breathing in from the base of your spine, drawing the breath up and circulating it throughout your body and exhaling out the top of your head. Continue *simultaneous breathing*, inhaling and exhaling, as the currents of energy enter from the base of your spine and the top of your head, spiraling around each other as they transit your chakra system in opposite directions and are released back out into the cosmos and down into the earth.

Notice the sensation of electricity flowing through your body, like a circuit reconnected to its power source. Feel yourself becoming one with the flow … and from this state of flow, allow yourself to travel through a rift in the fabric of time, stepping through a portal and out into an otherworldly cavern filled with multicolored light.

As your vision adjusts to the radiant light surrounding you, notice an image hovering directly in front of your eyes, indistinct in a pink mist. It appears to be a young child. As the form approaches, you recognize yourself in a much earlier time, at an age where you believed in the magic of life and you still knew everything was possible.

You find yourself charmed by the child that you were. … She is simply lovely, surrounded by the energy of childhood, abounding with adventure and mystery. Excitedly she extends her small hand to you, and taking it, you draw her close, recapturing a sense of wholeness you have not felt for a long time. She has much she wants to share with you about her life, her passions, and her dreams. You bask in her intoxicating energy, reveling in its innocence and promise. With the sweetest smile, she looks into your eyes, and without any effort at all, she slips into your heart chakra, where she fits perfectly.

Allow yourself to savor the lighthearted joy now safely tucked into your heart. (Pause.)

Walking farther now through shafts of brilliant orange and gold light, you become aware you are no longer alone, as another feminine form glides toward you through the thin veils of consciousness. Glowing with the flush of young womanhood, her exquisite gown and lush hair cascade around her. She is radiant with feminine beauty. She embraces you without reserve, her purity and composure a balm to your soul. Allow yourself the gift of receiving her fully, inhaling her essence … recognizing it as your own. Notice your senses liven in her presence, your desires and goals drawing into focus. With a knowing glance and a wink of her eye, she steps lightly into your heart chakra and settles herself there.

Turning now, fully entranced, you see in the green, leafy distance a third figure gracefully making its way across the clearing. Her countenance is shrouded in mystery, appearing beautiful and seductive one moment and ancient and wise the next. In her face, you see the face of your own elder self. In her eyes, a sense of peace from the acknowledgment of one's own coming of age. The gemstones around her neck refract the light, casting shadows of deep greens and blues into the hallowed space around her. She is mother, wife, sister, teacher, mentor—she is her own sovereign.

Gratefully, you allow yourself to be drawn to her as together you begin again *simultaneous breathing* … drawing your breath from the top of your head and the base of your spine at the same time, allowing the breath to move in opposite directions through your body, and then, out. … Feel the electric current spiraling along your spine as it entwines your two bodies as one. Continue simultaneous breathing until you sense the integration is complete. (Pause.)

In your expanded state, you now realize it is time to return and begin the process of transporting yourself back to your ordinary reality. Breathing easily and bringing your integrated selves with you, step back through the portal in time. Taking the care needed, gently reenter your physical form, allowing your own natural breath to return. When you are ready, open your eyes. Welcome back to our expanded sisterhood!

Closing Quote: On Sexuality
(Clarissa Pinkola Estes, excerpts from *Women Who Run with the Wolves*)

> The sacred and the sensual/sexual live very near one another in the psyche, for they are all brought to attention through a sense of wonder, not from intellectualizing but through experiencing something through the physical pathways of the body, something that for the moment or forever, whether it is a kiss, a vision, a belly laugh, or whatever, changes us, shakes us out, takes us to a pinnacle, smooths out our lines, gives us a dance step, a whistle, a true burst of life.
>
> In the sacred, the obscene, the sexual, there is always a wild laugh waiting ... Laughter is the hidden side of women's sexuality; it is physical, elemental, passionate, vitalizing, and therefore arousing. It is a kind of sexuality that does not have a goal. It is a sexuality of joy. [42]

---

[42] Clarissa Pinkola Estes, excerpts from *Women Who Run with the Wolves* (New York, NY: Penguin Random House, 1992), chapter 11.

❧

Week 29

Inquiry: Sex as Potentiality

Last week, we briefly explored the immense terrain of sexuality. This week, let us consider sexuality as *a component of Love*.

In *Talking Tao, Talk #1*, Osho has said that "when love expresses through you, it first expresses as the body. It becomes sex. If it expresses through the mind, which is higher, deeper, subtler, then it is called Love. If it expresses through the spirit, it becomes Prayer."[43]

Sex by itself is a physical drive, very animal. It has the capacity to grow into love if one becomes conscious and meditative. Through loving deeply, sex can be transformed into a bridge, a dance of the beyond. And within deep loving is contained the seed of compassion. Add meditation to love, and the essence of compassion is released.

What have been your experiences on the love continuum? Where do you usually reside? What hindrances, hurdles, or breakthroughs have you encountered in your efforts to navigate the rapids of sexuality and love?

How do your physical, mental, emotional, and spiritual bodies influence your journey?

Breathlessly …

---

[43] Osho, *Talking Tao, Talk #1.*

Meditation: What Love Is

Close your eyes and take three long, slow breaths. … As you exhale, feel your body relax, releasing all the tensions of your day. Notice the electric thrum continuously coursing up and down your spine like a current of light. Allow your consciousness to focus on this light as it moves from the top of your head down to the base of your spine, briefly pooling itself there before it moves effortlessly down into the earth, making its way toward the center of the planet, where it attaches itself like a lifeline. Connected now by this cord of golden silver light, you find yourself floating, weightless. Become conscious of the darkness behind your eyes as it deepens and begins pulling you in.

Relax in the emptiness. Allow it to seep into your body, your mind, until it is the only thing you are aware of—just you and the nothingness—no visuals, no sound to interrupt this profound sense of emptiness. Floating, effortlessly, you wait in the infinite void, open and receptive, your spine undulating ever so slightly, like a great fish slowly fanning its tail.

From this place of serene peace, you become aware of faint but intensely beautiful music originating from deep inside your own being. And listening intently, you hear the delicate notes of a divinely simple melody, like a single hand playing the higher octaves on a piano. The composition is alluring, and you feel your etheric body responding to the ancient and familiar melody as its song pours forth from within you and out into the void, like moonbeams casting their silver light out into the night sky.

As the music enlightens your senses, it provokes in you a longing to know the whole melody, to hear its extended harmonies. And listening even more deeply, you perceive a new strand of sound— this time pulsing toward you from the beyond. Its chords are resonant and rhythmic, and you recognize them as complementary to the melody already emanating from within you—their lower frequencies mingling with your higher frequencies. Out of the vast emptiness that now feels quite alive with intent born from the fusion of the inner and outer, a sacred symphony arises and fills the space around you.

Held aloft on the waves of exquisite sound, you find yourself drenched in shafts of the sun's brilliant golden light, filling you with wonder and warmth, its creative force alive with infinite possibilities. As the music crescendos and falls, moving from one interlude to another, the golden radiance of the sun yields to the silver glow of your moonlight, allowing a perpetual balancing of the light. And you find yourself buoyed with a profound sense of expansion and fulfillment.

Allow yourself to savor this state of completeness … (Pause.)

Gradually, you become conscious of your body as it gently tugs against the silver and gold cord still firmly fastened to the center of the earth. With a great sense of gratitude for the light and the music, which are now fully integrated within your whole being, you carefully take the cord in your hand and begin slowly pulling yourself back to ordinary space and time.

Unhurried, and mindful of reentering your physical body with care, bring yourself back to your place in the great circle of love awaiting you … and when you are ready, open your eyes. … Welcome back, beloveds.

Closing Quote: If You Can Be Meditative in Your Sex Life
(Osho, excerpt from *The Book of Wisdom*, Talk #7)

> Holding the hand of your woman or man, why not sit silently? Why not close your eyes and feel? Feel the presence of the other, enter into the presence of the other, let the other's presence enter into you; vibrate together, sway together; if suddenly a great energy possesses you, dance together—and you will reach to such orgasmic peaks of joy as you have never known before. Those orgasmic peaks have nothing to do with sex, in fact they have much to do with silence.
>
> And if you can also manage to become meditative in your sex life, if you can be silent while making love, in a kind of dance, you will be surprised. You have a built-in process to take you to the farthest shore. [44]

---

[44] Osho, excerpt "Talk #7," from *The Book of Wisdom: The Heart of Tibetan Buddhism* (Zurich, Switzerland: Osho International Foundation, 1984).

Week 30

Inquiry: Self-Limiting Beliefs—
Honoring Our Own Best Efforts

Self-imposed limitations are magnificently effective! In exploring self-limiting behaviors and beliefs and learning to move beyond them, it is essential to view yourself and your old patterns from a broader perspective. Seeing with new awareness, we can more deeply understand their etiology and acknowledge their original intent.

Almost always, our efforts to care for ourselves reflect our then-best abilities to successfully navigate the rapids of the rivers of our lives. Choose a particular limiting belief, or cluster of beliefs, and transport yourself back to the genesis of those beliefs. Let's take a look at how we came to adopt them and why they seemed like a good idea at the time.

- Where were you in your life when you adopted the behavior or belief?

- What was your original goal, intent, or purpose? How did you hope for it to promote your well-being or resolve your dilemma?

- Are you now able to recognize the pattern at its onset, or do you usually see it after the cycle has completed?

- How or when did you realize this pattern had become a hindrance?

- What are the payoffs and the penalties for staying in this loop and how has it shaped your life so far?

This evening, as we prepare to release these old patterns, let us honor the efforts of our earlier selves. Sorting through the detritus of what you now recognize as impeding your forward movement, excavate the hidden insights and buried gems that lie among the rubble. Retrieve these treasures, as they are gifts from your earlier self, and let the rest go.

Meditation: When We Were Young

As you settle yourself this evening, imagine bringing your childhood stuffed animal with you, a favorite toy or object that reminds you of yourself at an early age, and prepare to travel back to a time of innocence, a time when each morning promised the greatest adventures and you were in love with life. Close your eyes and see the girl you once were. See how adorable and trusting you were. If this was not the situation in your childhood, envision the girl you would have liked to have been, the life you would have wished for her. Listen to your own breath passing effortlessly in and out of your lungs, grounding you as you slip back through the illusion of time.

The atmosphere surrounding you is becoming progressively less and less dense … and you experience a very pleasant sense of weightlessness as you slowly merge into the picture in your mind. You find yourself floating right in front of her, the girl that was you so long ago … and leaning down, you gaze directly into her clear, unguarded eyes. Observe her features, the color and texture of her hair, her sweet child smell; see the joy that beams from her laughing eyes when she smiles at you, charming you in that way children do, as you feel yourself being slowly drawn into her.

Within her, you find yourself enveloped in a softly radiant space, wrapped by a sense of simple grace. The purity of her intentions whispers over you like gossamer, gentle as a feather. You find yourself wondering, how long has it has been since you basked in such an uncomplicated state of well-being? Allow yourself to relax into this safe space. Feel a tingle of excitement in the depths of your heart as a fluttering of faith begins to take flight, like a nestling. (Pause.)

As you continue to intertwine yourself with this child who is still an aspect of you, images begin to flow through your mind, bringing a deep comprehension of her heart, the purity of her world, her unquestioned trust in the overriding power of good. You can literally feel the brilliance of the light she carries. Unequivocally, you know that every effort she makes, her every breath is founded in the purity of love.

And as this understanding grows, it begins to integrate itself within you, bringing with it the evolution of your own self–understanding as an adult, a profound recognition that at your core, you too are faultless and good. You know that her choices and your choices have always emanated from the intention to do good.

Take some time to allow this transformational realization to deepen, realigning the many selves you carry within. … Relax into it fully. … (Pause.)

As your adult self begins to slip back through the veils of time, allow yourself to retain the lightness you have experienced with your child self. Feel yourself reenter your human form, slowly settling into your physical body, bringing your awareness back to your room. Gently begin moving your toes and your fingers and allow your etheric eyes to make contact with your sisters sitting in the sacred women's circle around you. Slowly open your eyes. Welcome back!

Closing Quotes: Release the Familiar
(Alan Cohen)

> It takes a lot of courage to release the familiar and seemingly secure, to embrace the new. But there is no real security in what is no longer meaningful. There is more security in the adventurous and exciting, for in movement there is life, and in change, there is power.
>
> And after you have made your commitment to say no to what no longer serves you, you will probably be invited to demonstrate that you really mean it. [45]

---

[45] Alan Cohen, BrainyQuote.com.

Week 31

Inquiry: Using Our Resources to Transmute Limitation

This week, we look a bit further and deeper into yet another facet of our self-limiting patterns—their *antidotes*.

What medicine, what allies seen and unseen, what skills and talents are present in your life to support you in your intention to transmute and transform these limiting patterns and beliefs?

Now is the time to create the opportunity to explore and reclaim the resources already existing and available to us in our lives. What do you find, and how will you use them? When?

Meditation: Power Animal Meditation

Find an inviting place to sit on the floor or lie comfortably on your bed. … Allow yourself to become still. Close your eyes. Breathe deeply and slowly, relaxing all your muscles. See your crown chakra as a large orb filled with the most divine white light energy. Now visualize a cord of this very same light energy flowing from your crown chakra down through the top of your head, traveling along the course of your spine all the way down to the earth beneath you … and moving down even farther, deep into the center of the planet, connecting with its molten core. Feel the warm energy of the earth as it begins flowing up through this cord of light and into your body resting above. Allow this energy and power to surge through you until you can feel a tingling from your feet to your head. Relax into this tingling sensation and allow the darkness behind your eyelids to envelop you like a wave.

Visualize yourself walking through a silver mist, making your way along a winding path and just beyond until you come upon a secret doorway to another realm. Cautiously slipping over the threshold, you find yourself gazing upon the most beautiful, lush landscape that extends as far as the eye can see. Step out into it. … Allow yourself to visually explore the wonder that surrounds you. What kind of place are you in? (Pause.)

Eventually, an image begins to take shape in the distance, moving toward you. As it comes into focus, you recognize the form of an animal totem. Prepare yourself to honor the presence of one of your spirit guides, allowing whatever time it may take for your spirit guide to feel comfortable enough to approach you. (Pause.)

What kind of animal is it? Is it from this world or some other realm? Acquaint yourself with your animal friend. … Allow any communication to happen naturally. (Pause.)

What does your spirit animal have to teach you? What power or magic does it carry? Become familiar with how it moves, how it communicates, how it manifests its own unique qualities and purpose.

You may wish to ask your spirit guide to walk with you, to be with you during a particular aspect of your life. You may ask to meet again, to get to know each other better. If it feels appropriate, you may wish to give your animal friend a gift, or to receive one … (Pause.)

When your spirit animal indicates to you that it is time to depart, thank him or her and, with great gratitude, bid farewell until your next meeting.

Now, slowly make your way back to the doorway and step out onto the pathway and into the silver mist. As the glow envelops your body, you feel the air shift and know that you are once again entering back into your ordinary reality, into your room where your physical body waits for your return, its light cord securely connected to the earth. Gently reenter your body. When you are ready, open your eyes and rejoin the sisterhood. Notice all the spirit guides and totems who have joined us this evening!

Closing Quotes: Two Seed Quotes

(Cynthia Occelli)

For a seed to achieve its greatest expression, it must come completely undone. The shell cracks, its insides come out, and everything changes. To someone who doesn't understand growth, it would look like complete destruction.

If you love beauty, it's because beauty lives within you. If you love art, it's because you are creative. If it wakes up your heart, a receptor for it already exists within you. Your soul is drawn to the things that will help you unfold your most glorious expression. Give in. [46]

---

[46] Cynthia Occelli, quotes from Goodreads.com.

Week 32

Inquiry: The Back Door of Being in Process

Consider some aspect of your life about which you have not yet arrived at a clear and committed choice, some matter about which you find yourself keeping the back door of your decision ajar. Ponder the following:

- Are you more comfortable being in process than arriving at a solution or destination?

- When you make a decision, do you reconsider it and continue to wonder whether it was the right choice? Or do you embrace it and move forward without looking back?

- Do you feel entitled to manifest what you want in your life? Do you live your life in alignment with your belief?

- Do you confuse contemplation with procrastination?

- How comfortable are you with group decisions?

Until we meet in the evening hours …

Meditation: Returning Full Circle

Let's enter the evening by settling our minds. … Begin a gentle rhythm of equalized breathing, balancing your inhaling and exhaling breaths. … Release your thoughts, allowing them to fade away. … Feel your body fully relax and begin to expand slightly as if stretching the space surrounding it. And within this new spaciousness, feel yourself begin to float, weightless, up into the ethers, tethered securely to the core of the planet by your trusty silver cord.

You float upward until you find yourself enshrouded within a thick, dense mist of gold and silver light. Feel the damp, warm particles of the atmosphere caress your body, massaging you, channeling their light into the deepest recesses of your being. As you surrender yourself to this gold and silver cloud, you become aware of how depleted you have become ... and in your expanded form, you open yourself even further to the healing energies of this delicious light. Relax now and allow yourself to be fully recharged. (Pause.)

Incubating in the cocoon of healing energies, you gradually realize you are surrounded by several vague and dimly colored orbs; hovering expectantly around you, they seem to wait. Reaching out, you beckon to them, inviting them to come closer, and as you open your heart chakra, one by one they enter into the vast chamber of your heart. As they enter, their colors begin to regain their intensity, eventually filling the cavities of your heart chakra with brilliant, saturated light. Feel your heart expand as it welcomes home these traveling orbs. Breathe deeply, absorbing the vibrant colors as they circulate throughout your whole body from the top of your head to the tips of your fingers and toes.

Now, in a state of complete fulfillment, you gaze up wonderingly, and in the distant sky, you see the full circle of the moon, that feminine goddess of the night. Bright and reflective, she dances in the sky, very grand in her domain, emanating an iridescent shaft of light across the darkness. And as her light beckons, you realize the moon is drawing you to her across the infinity of space and time. Deep in your belly, you feel the flutter of your own response to her call and find yourself eager to go to her. As you approach the moon, you realize her resplendence and her power. And in much the same way as the orbs merged back into you, you attach your own silver thread to the moon and allow yourself to be drawn into her ... and you fall together.

Full moon, full cycle ... your vessel is completely full and pregnant with the unmanifest, with unbounded possibility, with unrealized potential. Take this moment to embrace the goddess of the moon. Called *Selene* in Greek and *Luna* in Latin, the goddess is the personification of the moon itself, reflecting its feminine vibration on all who live on planet Earth. (Pause.)

101

When you are ready, prepare to transport yourself back through time and space to our ordinary reality. As you enter your physical form, create the appropriate space for the colors, the light, and the healing energies you have gathered on your spirit journey this evening. Vow to honor your renewed connection with the moon goddess, embracing her qualities of receptivity and intuition. Again, begin rhythmic, equalized breathing—inhaling and exhaling in balance as you bring yourself fully back to your room and to the sisterhood that surrounds you there. Welcome back.

Closing Quote: Learning from the Stones
(Sue Patton Thoele from *The Woman's Book of Spirit*)

> Time and trouble will tame an advanced young woman, but an advanced old woman is uncontrollable by any earthly force.

> Yes, and for the good of the whole, we *need* to be uncontrollable, and untamed, in our efforts to invite the spirit of love to quench the thirst of our souls and re-green our world.

> Gleaning wisdom from indigenous and eastern cultures who revere their elders, we can often glimpse the beauty of aging as exemplified by Nature … the awesome beauty created by the eons-old rock that adapted to the elements and over the millennium, grew a window through which the pristine sky gleams. In the face of her patient transformation, from one kind of beauty to another, we find ourselves asking:

> - How can I mature as I age?
> - What sandy sediment within me needs to erode away?
> - What window into my very soul is yearning to be revealed in my walled-in personal world?
> - What must be transformed in me in order for my transparency to reveal a vast and changing sky?

I have no answers—only the knowledge that they will come if I remain open to the questions![47]

---

[47] Reproduced with permission from Sue Patton Thoele, *The Women's Book of Spirit* (Berkeley, CA: Conari Press, 2006).

Week 33

Inquiry: Imbolc

Imbolc—the celebration of the light, also called *Candlemas*—is celebrated halfway between the winter solstice and the spring equinox. The word *Imbolc* is Gaelic for "in the belly." This is the holy day for honoring the return of the light, claiming the life, the *new* that longs to grow *in* you and *through* you … claiming it, saying yes to it, manifesting it with intention and blessing.

What fertile seed is beginning to grow down in the belly of your deepest being? We all know it can be delicious riding the wave of infinite potentials, keeping our options open. And then there comes that moment to shift out of the void, to grab hold of your dream and leap with it into the real.

It's time to initiate. Time to let the light shine through you.

Last week, we agreed to close our back doors and to live in alignment with our commitments. In the time since then, what have you discovered about your front door? Is it open and receptive? Have you noticed any shifts or changes wanting to be made? What naturally occurring movement has been initiated, and how can you fuel the fire, nourish the seed?

Meditation: Communing with an Orb

This evening, once again begin a gentle rhythm of equalized breathing, balancing your incoming and outgoing breaths, breathing slowly and deeply. … Relax. Dropping your silver cord down deep into the earth and fastening it there, imagine yourself floating in the darkness of the galaxy. Emerging from the depths, you recognize the minor planet Vesta, the brightest asteroid, keeper of your own personal, sacred flame, that little light inside you that makes you special. As she passes by in her orbit, a small spark leaps across the void and plunges into the depths of your solar plexus, tucking itself into you. Her flame is lunar energy, the brilliant, reflected fire of moonlight. Feeling the comforting flicker of this creative warmth, you drift on ...

In the distance hangs the moon, our silver goddess of the night. Taking hold of her iridescent shaft of light, you pull yourself closer and closer until you are fully in her presence, bathed in her silent beauty. Resting together, you feel yourself relax, and you begin to open your heart. As the space around your heart expands, you can see into the vast cavern that is your heart chakra ... and there, rotating, casting their light about the chamber, you see many brightly colored orbs. You recall that orbs frequently carry an aspect of our selves that has been neglected, or become lost or invisible. And you recognize these orbs from a time when your own inner light was depleted and dim. But the orbs sought their way home again, and now glowing brightly, they have become reintegrated ... a natural part of your being. You feel protective of them, and as well, somewhat curious.

One orb in particular attracts your attention, and as you watch, it slows and approaches you, allowing you to study its features. You notice its size and shape, and you see the deep hues of its color now glowing so strongly. You can feel its texture and taste its atmosphere. Suddenly you have a desire to enter this orb. You begin looking for a point of entry—a hole, a rip in its surface, an invitation. In response, the orb quietly opens itself to you. What does it feel like inside? Is there a sense of purpose or message? Perhaps it has a connection to a memory or earlier time in your life. What does it represent to you now? Be with this lesser-known aspect of your energy and allow yourself to enjoy a sense of peace with it. (Pause.)

When you feel your communing together has come to a completion, bring yourself once again to its outer surface. Gazing with affection and acceptance upon this reclaimed part of yourself, you watch with fascination as it immediately begins to condense into a tiny spot of brilliant light, and in a flash, it is drawn directly into your solar plexus, joining with the sacred flame from Vesta that already burns there.

Feeling lit with a new sense of integration and well-being, you begin to make your way back to your body with its silver cord still securely fastened to the core of the earth … and being careful not to bruise, you begin the transition from your expanded etheric form back into your more contracted physical body, which fits perfectly! You feel happy to be back. When you are fully grounded, open your eyes. Welcome back!

This evening, we delve deeper into our ability to live within our commitments, to actually germinate our seeds of creation. The talking stick is now held aloft …

Closing Quote: Creativity
(Osho, excerpts from *Creativity: Unleashing the Forces Within*)

True art means if it helps you to become silent, still, joyous; if it gives you a celebration, if it makes you dance—whether anybody participates with you or not is irrelevant. If it becomes a bridge between you and God, that is true art. If it becomes a meditation, that is true art. If you become absorbed in it, so utterly absorbed that the ego disappears, that is true art.

Life is an opportunity to create meaning. Meaning has not to be discovered: it has to be created. You will find meaning only if you create it. It is not there like a rock that you will find. It is a poetry to be composed, it is a song to be sung, it is a dance to be danced. [48]

---

[48] Osho, excerpts from *Creativity: Unleashing the Forces Within* (New York, NY: St Martin's Griffin, Osho International Foundation, 1999), pages 169, 170, 181.

Week 34

Inquiry: Allure of the Old Ways

Are there areas of your life in which *the old ways no longer work*? Are you holding on to treasured or inherited beliefs, philosophies, material possessions, habits, customs—even definitions of yourself that no longer serve your best interests? Do you experience a sense of being out of touch, drained, or ineffective and wonder why?

Oftentimes as we move into new phases of our lives, we take with us the old tools, the old perceptions, and the old expectations that have been our allies in the past. Our new movement forward may have been created by our own intentional evolution; or it may be the result of changes in the world around us over which we have little control. We may be conscious of these changes or completely unaware of them, in denial even.

How do you know when it is time to release the old and embrace the new? What significance does tradition, loyalty, or saving face hold for you? Are you effective at recognizing, in the moment, when you are returning to the old? Are you capable of intercepting your own process to introduce and honestly embrace the new?

This week, let's go beyond theoretical discussion and move to the roots. Relying on the sanctuary of our circle and its gentle support, choose one or more areas you suspect, or know, fits this description. Share with us how this negatively impacts your life.

Meditation: Lotus Lagoon

Bring yourself into a state of deep peace and serenity, balancing your incoming and outgoing breath, inhaling and exhaling, using equalized breathing. Drop a silver cord deep down into the earth as you allow your spirit body to rise and gently drift through the open window that has just appeared on your left. You find yourself floating effortlessly out into the warm night … moving toward a wooded glen beyond the trees. There is a beam of moonlight following you, lighting your way from behind, and you can see your shadow in front of you as you move down the path … your exact twin. See how beautiful she is!

In the dusky clearing, you come upon a lagoon shimmering in the night, mist rising into the darkness. Lightning bugs hover in the night air, reflected like fallen stars in the mirrored surface of the pool. … The water is deep and covered in shades of green and purple, an infinity of shiny leaves. You realize these are the leaves of the sacred lotus, its tuberous roots buried deep in the luscious mud of Mother Earth. Smoothly veined leaves spiral upward, unfurling into gently rounded and very broad cups, overflowing with night dew.

Irresistibly, you are drawn to the edge of the lagoon and find yourself moving into the water … sinking slowly down until you are submerged, warm water embracing you, smooth as liquid silk, and there you bathe in the moonlight among a garden of lotus leaves, your feet in soft mud.

Gazing across the surface of the pool, you notice for the first time a multitude of flowers … white and pink, some with fuchsia tips, golden centers borne on stalks high above the surface, all pointing up; each of their petals is covered with dew drops … and captured within each individual drop, you see the reflections of the moon glowing like luminous pearls.

As you lie floating, the surrounding leaves move closer until you are enfolded in the green tapestry of leaves and blossoms. Reaching out, you dip your fingers into the leaf cups of dew and gently begin rubbing it onto your face and neck, through your hair, down your arms and over your breasts … anointing your skin with the dew collected by the lotus leaves in the moonlight.

Then, reaching to the nearest lotus blossoms, you carefully pluck the pearls of moonlight from their centers, and stringing them on a moonbeam, you place them on the crown of your head where they lay like a wreathe, emitting the softest harmonies that fill the night with the vibration of celestial music.

Eventually, you become aware that much time has passed. The moon has dipped low on the horizon, her light barely visible through the trees, and from the shore, your shadow beckons.

Empowered by the lunar halo around your head and the ethereal melodies in the air, you make your way back to the path, leaving the forest to the night. You notice with some gratitude that the window to your room awaits you and slip easily through its opening to merge with your physical form once again, bringing with you all the dew and the music and the radiance from your night, to be assimilated into your ordinary reality.

When you feel stable and grounded once again, allow your body to begin to move slightly, wiggling your fingers and toes and on up into your core until you feel comfortably reintegrated. Slowly open your eyes. Welcome back!

Closing Quote: Inguz
(Ralph Blum, excerpt from the "8ᵗʰ Rune, Inguz: Fertility, New Beginnings, Ing, the Hero God," *Book of Runes*)

> All things change, and we cannot live permanently amid obstructions. Inguz signals your emergence from a closed chrysalis state. As you resolve and clear away the old, you will experience a release from tension and uncertainty.
>
> You may be required to free yourself from a rut, a habit or relationship, from some deep cultural or behavioral pattern, some activity that was quite proper to the self you are leaving behind. The time of birth is always a critical one. Movement can involve danger, and yet movement that is timely leads out of danger. Enter the delivery room now.

Another of the Cycle Runes, Inguz counsels preparation. Being centered and grounded, freeing yourself from all unwanted influences and seeing the humor, you are indeed prepared to open yourself to the will of Heaven and await your deliverance with calm certainty. [49]

---

[49] Ralph Blum, excerpt from "Inguz the 8th Rune: Fertility, New Beginnings, Ing the Hero God," from *Book of Runes* (New York, NY: Harper Collins Publishers, 2000).

Week 35

Inquiry: Choose One!

Following last week's call wherein we identified specific areas of our lives ripe for change—outmoded beliefs, philosophies, material possessions, habits, customs, even self-definitions—this week we pursue part two of the process of freeing ourselves from the old and familiar.

Defying the old adage, *when everything is said and done, there's a lot more said than done,* choose one of your old, outworn paradigms. Make it a significant one, one you are determined to release or transform.

What action or movement will you commit to doing in order to shift this old pattern or dilemma? What are the specific steps necessary to actually implement the change?

Okay, now do it! And tell us how it went.

See you in the sanctuary …

Meditation: The Golden Kochyli

Bringing yourself to a state of rest, begin equalized breathing, slowly inhaling and exhaling … dropping your golden cord down to the center of the earth and fastening it there. Close your eyes and begin to hear the soft sounds of waves as they crash on the shore of a distant beach. Allow the deep tones of the water to reverberate in your inner ear as the vibrations move deeper and deeper into your core, transporting you to the sand. (Pause.) Here on the beach, there is a light breeze that caresses your face, and the late-afternoon sun warms your body. ... Smell the sea air. Feel the salt and the sand on your skin. As you gaze across the waters, you notice the sun is heading down toward the horizon as it prepares to drop into the ocean for the night.

Strolling along the beach, your feet playfully wander through beds of ocean debris strewn with seaweed—collections of shells, driftwood, an occasional gull feather, fanciful piles of sea life abandoned by the receding tides. Glancing farther down the beach, you notice an object as it rolls lazily back into the sea, only to be picked up by the next incoming wave and tossed emphatically up onto the tawny sand, where it again begins to roll back down to the water.

Intrigued, you make your way to the place where it disappeared beneath the surface, and there in the shallows you can see a sparkling golden form with multiple rounded points on one end. ... It appears to be a large and beautiful shell. Just as you reach down to pick it up, a towering wall of dark turquoise water rises up in front of you, sucking the golden shell up into its watery depths as it gathers momentum. Turning quickly and scrambling back toward the shore, you feel the water hurl itself at your backside ... soaking your hair, your shoulders, streaming down the backs of your legs, washing your whole body in a delicious baptism of sea water, warm and frothy, sticky with salt. It feels so refreshing! Struggling to maintain your balance in the tumbling waters, you clamber up the wet sand, laughing, and flop down onto the beach, where you begin to squeeze the water from your hair and rub the salt all over your arms and legs to dry in the setting sun. You feel a tremendous sense of gratitude for this gift from the sea, reminding you of the infinite abundance of the ocean and the healing powers in the joy of the beach. With deep gratitude, you relax into it.

The setting sun is now almost to the horizon, painting the darkening sky with deep pinks and purples, and the tides have continued their retreat farther into the ocean. You know that it is time for you to go. As you arise, lying a bit farther down on the sand abandoned by the tides, is the golden shell—a beautiful Kochyli, its spiral shape opening into a flared, golden whorl with opalescent colors along its edges. Picking it up and carefully placing its aperture to your ear, you hear from its depths the sounds of oceanic waves gently and endlessly caressing distant shores.

The soothing sounds bring you a deep sense of peace and a knowing that all is exactly as it should be. A magnificent treasure from the sea, this shell carries forever the sounds of the waves, of new life arriving upon your shores … washing away the old.

Holding the shell to your heart, you begin to make your way back to the place in the sand where you first entered this beach. … And following the footprints that were yours, you retrace your steps back to your room to find yourself sitting in a circle of beautiful women, surrounded by the smell of sea air and great contentment and gaiety. Gently settle into yourself and when you are fully returned to your physical form, lay your shell by your side and open your eyes. Welcome back!

Closing Quote: The Beauty We Love (Rumi)

> Let the beauty we love be what we do. There are hundreds of ways to kneel and kiss the ground. [50]

---

[50] Rumi quote, public domain.

Week 36

Inquiry: How Does Your Garden Grow?

It seems fitting, after our weeks of searching for and then sowing the seeds of new ways to live and new selves to cultivate, to now inquire how your gardens grow. Any new shoots yet? Have you noticed any companion plants sprouting up alongside your intended crops? How about weeds?

This week, come prepared to share your stories of how it is, having released your old and familiar, while you await the arrival of the new.

And congratulations on trusting your own process. Spring is just around the corner!

Meditation: Mud-Luscious Meditation

Bring yourself into a comfortable seated position, relaxing your body by breathing deeply three times. Send your etheric roots down deep into the earth, fastening them there with a thin silver cord. Begin equalized breathing, bringing in the light energy up from the earth, balancing your inhaling and exhaling breath, allowing your breathing to become deeper and slower as you relax into the rhythm. (Pause.) Now, take a deep breath in and hold it gently as you contract your root chakra. Feel and visualize the light energy spiraling its way up your spine all the way to your crown chakra, holding it there for a few moments and then exhaling it back down your spinal column again and out the bottoms of your feet. Keep your equalized breathing slow and even. Again, draw in a deep breath, contract your base chakra, and send the light energy up the entire length of your spine into your crown, spiraling it around and then back down and out your feet, deep into the earth to be neutralized. You may begin to feel less congested as you breathe away the toxins and blockages that have been held in your body. Savor this new sense of opening and clarity.

It is very early spring. Much of the nature kingdom still slumbers beneath a soft blanket of snow, and a new moon hangs hidden in the predawn sky. In the near distance, you find yourself staring at a large mineral tufa, shrouded by clouds of hot steam arising from a small pool below, nestled among layers of smooth stone. As you come closer, you can see frothy water bubbling up through cracks in the earth as if from geothermal aquifers deep beneath the surface. An earthy mineral scent fills the air as the steamy vapors caress your body with their wet warmth, enticing you into the hot, bubbly water.

As you slip into the pool, you immediately realize you are not alone ... and although you cannot see them, you know you are surrounded by beings from the spirit realm. You sense tremendous benevolence and love here. Feeling completely at ease, you allow your body to sink farther down into the crystalline spring waters. And as dawn creeps above the horizon and throws soft pinks and blues across the heavens, the surface of the water reflects the colors of the new day in perfect symmetry: as above, so below. Allowing your eyes to close, let go into a profound sense of being held ... (Pause.) ... floating in the pool, warm, wet, weightless, safe.

As you float, begin sensing deep into your physical body, becoming conscious of those places where your emotional or physical mud remains congealed or congested. And reaching down, imagine that you are scooping up some warm, healing mud from the bottom of the pool and placing it over the congested areas, gently rubbing it in, allowing the healing mud of the pool to loosen and mix with the congested mud of yourself.

Feel the muds integrate and eventually dissolve as they disappear altogether into the slow-moving currents of the pool. Continue applying more mud to those areas of your body that seek relief, massaging it in ... allowing mud to absorb mud and then dissolve ... until you feel complete for now. (Pause.)

Become aware of the tremendous gratitude pouring out from your heart, for the renewed sense of healing and purity now coursing through your whole being. And remember to offer thanks to the healing waters and its mud.

Now you begin the process of returning from your journey, once again becoming aware of your physical form. Slowly open your eyes. See the candlelight flickering in the corner of your room and the glowing faces of the mud-luscious women sitting in the circle around you. Welcome back!

Closing Quotes: You Were Born with Potential
(Rumi)

You were born with potential.
You were born with goodness and trust. You were born with ideals and dreams.
You were born with greatness.
You were born with wings.
You are not meant for crawling, so don't.
You have wings.
Learn to use them and fly.

Yesterday I was clever, so I wanted to change the world.
Today I am wise, so I am changing myself. [51]

---

[51] Rumi quote, public domain.

∽

Week 37

Inquiry: Typologies as Tools

Countless typologies found within the arts and sciences of exploring consciousness can become valuable tools in the quest for existential knowledge of ourselves and others. Astrology, the study of archetypes, the enneagram, human design systems and the gene keys, numerology, psychology, integral theory, and multitudes more all become powerful allies in illuminating the paths that may otherwise remain undiscovered, unrecognized, or even rejected.

Considering any of the life-altering decisions upon which you have mused, currently or in the past, what typologies have you found helpful in moving toward wise choices for your emerging self?

Share with us, if you will, the inside process of how that typology cast new or different light on your options, your perceptions, and your understanding of them and of yourself. What might be the pitfalls of relying on typologies?

Meditation: Green Light Meditation

Allow your body to sit or recline in a restful position with your spine straight, your hands resting at your sides. Take a few moments to quiet the mind, slow your breath, and ground yourself into the evening … into our circle. Gazing into the center of the circle, feel the power pulsating there. … Close your eyes … (Pause.)

Visualize a beautiful emerald-green flame before you and begin drawing it into the center of your being—to the healing space surrounding your heart, expanding it with each breath. Allow this flame to grow until it envelops you in a beautiful sphere of shimmering, emerald light energy. Feel the love, the warmth, and the healing energy from this green flame radiating out from your heart center and permeating every facet of your body. Let it warm your heart and cleanse your being, healing any wounds and replenishing any loss … (Pause.)

Now, holding this green light in your heart, begin channeling this loving, healing light out onto the earth in order that it may be a balm to the spirits of all who call this planet home. See the light pierce the veil of darkness that blankets the planet, bringing light and hope from the beyond into our world.

Bring your focus to that place you call your residence and begin to see the green light unfurl itself until it completely envelops your home, expanding ever farther, more brilliant until it has encompassed your city and then your country with heart light energy … and expanding even beyond until you can see the entire planet surrounded by a beautiful mist of shimmering emerald–green light, floating, pulsating, glowing with its message of love as it soars out into the universe.

See all living beings, every woman, man, and child, and the animal and plant kingdoms, opening to the healing warmth of the green heart light. Let it raise the consciousness of all that it touches, creating a world of harmonious unity and kindness, a planet of beneficence and grace.

Be with the green light … breathe it, bathe yourself in it … and feel the oneness that is possible. Know that this is your natural state and allow it to penetrate you.

Immediately beneath you, sense the presence of your sisters, positioned around a single green flame that flickers still in the etheric center of a circle. Notice there is an open space waiting for you there and gently bring yourself back. (Pause.)

And with a sigh of gratitude, exhale as you whisper, "It is done."

When you are ready, open your eyes. Welcome back.

Linda Laws

Closing Quotes: Being Whole
(two quotes from Lawrence Anthony)

But perhaps the most important lesson I learned is that there are no walls between humans and the elephants except those that we put up ourselves, and that until we allow not only elephants, but all living creatures their place in the sun, we can never be whole ourselves.

Our inability to think beyond our own species, or to be able to co-habit with other life forms in what is patently a massive collaborative quest for survival, is surely a malady that pervades the human soul. [52]

---

[52] Lawrence Anthony, founder of Thula Thula, Private Game Reserve, Zululand, South Africa, author of *The Elephant Whisperer* (New York, NY: St. Martin's Press, 2009).

Week 38

Inquiry: Accessing the Laws of Abundance and Attraction

If we can forget for the moment our obsession with abundance and allow our focus to simply be on the attainment of a state of joy, we just might find it all flows from there. Once having attained a state of joy, the vibration of joy infuses our whole being. In essence, we will have reprogrammed our natural state to the frequency of joyousness.

By focusing attention on the heart of who we are, our whole being begins to vibrate more expansively. Then, since *like attracts like*, we draw to ourselves any and all things that are in sync with this expansive heart energy. (Abraham Hicks)

My dearest sisters, women in transition all, consider your relationship with two powerful and key dynamics: the laws of abundance and the laws of attraction. Come share with us what you find.

Meditation: Blossoming

Breathing easily and slowly, allow your energy to travel deep into the earth. When you have reached the center of the planet, drop your roots into the vast reservoir of shakti energy that resides there, grounding yourself. Visualize the light moving up from the center of the earth into your base chakra, warming and cleansing your roots, and then moving up through each of your chakras, illuminating, warming, and cleansing each one until the light finally reaches the top of your head. Opening your crown chakra, allow the light energy to flow out the top of your head like a fountain, flowing down and all around you in a shower of light enveloping your physical form, like an egg. Feel the egg shape enclose you in its soft and comfortable breathiness … sweet and clean, the energy of renewal.

Imagine yourself resting safely inside this egg lying deep in the fertile soil of the earth. Nearby, you can see new grasses and the first small blossoms as they make their way to the surface to be born and sway in the gentle breezes in their celebration of life. It is springtime. Butterflies and dragonflies abound in the air above you, and you can hear a symphony of birdsong … bees buzzing … the nature kingdom at its busiest, pollinating and building, a world of delicate wings sending their vibrations into the balmy air.

As you incubate in your egg, bring your awareness to the warmth of the soil surrounding you, which is filled with tiny insects, worms, and a multitude of just-waking seeds, bulbs, and tubers. An electric current of anticipation pulses around you, a sense of patience and impeccable timing waiting for the moment of rebirth. And then you begin to feel small rustlings and subtle movements around you as, one by one, seed shells are discarded and roots plunge down into the soil, tender shoots pushing their way up through the sun-warmed earth and out into the light of day. As you witness this gentle explosion of creativity, you suddenly realize that you too are filled with an abundance of seedlings and small shoots that are now breaking through their seed shells and making their way up toward your surface to emerge into the light. The meadow is blossoming. And so are you. Allow a sense of renewal to pervade your whole being as your body and your spirit are reborn. (Pause.)

It is now time to begin your return to ordinary reality. Remember with gratitude and appreciation the new life that slowly incubated within your egg state until it was time to be brought into your world, and realize that those blossoms are an integral part of you, an inner garden that you carry with you, always.

As you slip back into your physical form, slowly return your awareness to your room and to the sweet scent of spring blooms that surrounds you there. Settling into your physical form, ground yourself once again, and when you can feel your roots, open your eyes.

Closing Quote: You Came from a Source
(Dr. Wayne W. Dyer, excerpt from his Introduction to *Ask and It Is Given: Learning to Manifest Your Desires,* by Esther and Jerry Hicks)

The message here is quite startling and yet oh-so-simple—you came from a Source of love and well-being.

When you're matched up to that energy of peace and love, you then regain the power of your Source—the power to manifest your desires, to summon well-being, to attract abundance where scarcity previously resided, and to access Divine guidance in the form of the right people and the precisely correct circumstances.

This is what your Source does, and since you emanated from that Source, you can and will do the same. [53]

---

[53] Dr. Wayne W. Dyer, excerpt from his Introduction to *Ask and It Is Given: Learning to Manifest Your Desires,* by Esther and Jerry Hicks (Carlsbad, CA: Hay House, Inc. 2004).

Week 39

Inquiry: Dancing with Abundance and Attraction

As we learn to trust in the Laws of Attraction and Abundance, we can eventually come to trust that there is enough for all of us, and that we deprive no one with our abundance. But this concept seems to defy all we have been taught in our "survival of the fittest" world. We tend to think we need to go out and shake a few trees to make things happen, which is good. Action is necessary. However, it seldom seems to work in a linear fashion. Time and again, we may do the work of becoming internally clear and focused about our dreams and intentions, take a few outward steps in their direction, only to have a door flung open where you had no idea there even was a door.

—Julia Cameron, *The Artist's Way*[54]

Considering your own dance with abundance and attraction …

- Are you adept at recognizing an opportunity when it appears—even if it is in a different form than anticipated?

- Do you prefer to remain loyal to a preconceived notion of what your opportunity will look like?

- Are you capable of defining your *what* and being open to the *how* of it?

---

[54] Julia Cameron, excerpt from *The Artist's Way* (New York, NY: GP Putnam's Sons, 1992).

- What is your understanding of your role in the process of manifesting?

Pondering …

Meditation: Metta-Loving Kindness Meditation
(Joan Borysenko from *Pocketful of Miracles, Prayer Practice* for February 11–15, adapted for time)

Begin by taking a few letting-go breaths and then enter the divine sanctuary of stillness …
Imagine the light and love of Spirit pouring over you and washing through you, revealing the purity of your own heart. See this light extending beyond you and merging with the divine light.

And now, see yourself totally enclosed in an egg of light … and repeat these lovingkindness blessings for yourself:

May I be at peace, may my heart remain open,
May I awaken to the light of my own true nature;
May I be healed. May I be a source of healing for all things.
(Pause.)

Now visualize a loved one … seeing your beloved in your mind's eye in as much detail as possible. Imagine the light of Spirit washing through them, revealing the light within their heart. See this light grow brighter, merging with the divine light, enclosing them in an egg of light, and repeat these lovingkindness blessings for them:

May you be at peace, may your heart remain open,
May you awaken to the light of your own true nature;
May you be healed. May you be a source of healing for all things.
(Pause.)

Now, finally, visualize our beautiful planet enveloped in this divine light ~ the green continents, the blue waters, the white polar caps. The two-leggeds and four-leggeds, the fish that swim and the birds that fly … blessing them all:

May there be peace on Earth,
May the hearts of all beings be open to themselves and to each other;

May we all awaken to the light of our own true natures,
And may all creation be blessed and be a blessing to all that is.

Know that you can repeat these blessings of intention for yourself any time during the day – when you feel alone or are in doubt, or simply out of touch with the light within. (Pause.) [55]

Slowly now, begin to bring your awareness back to your body lying still … allowing your own natural breath to return. Slowly begin moving your fingers and toes, and when you are ready, open your eyes. Welcome back.

Closing Quotes: Living Life Backwards
(Margaret Young) and A Note from the Universe (Mike Dooley from tut.com)

Often people attempt to live their lives backwards:
they try to *have* more things,
or more money,
in order to *do* more of what they want … so that
they will *be* happier.

The way it actually works is the reverse:
You must first *be* who you really are,
then, *do* what you need to do,
in order to *have* what you truly want. (Margaret Young)[56]

Let's pretend, just for today, all day long, throughout our every thought and decision, that life is easy, that everyone means well, and that time is on our side. Okay?

And let's pretend that we are loved beyond belief, that magic conspires on our behalf, and that nothing can ever hurt us without our consent. Alright?

---

[55] Reproduced with permission from Joan Borysenko, adaptation of "Metta-Loving Kindness Meditation," from *Pocketful of Miracles Prayer Practice* (New York, NY: Warner Books, 1994).
[56] Margaret Young quote.

And if we like this game, we'll play tomorrow
as well,
and the next day,
and the next,
and pretty soon, it won't be a game at all,
because life, for us, will become those things.
Just as it's become what it is today.

Thoughts become things ... so remember to
choose the good ones!
Thoughts become worlds, too.
Visualize, every day ... and the earth will rock
and you will roll!

You're getting warmer. (Mike Dooley)[57]

---

[57] Reproduced with permission from Mike Dooley, *The Universe Talks*,
April 1, 2016, © www.tut.com.

Week 40

Inquiry: A Closer Look at *Money*

Abundance comes in many forms and guises. Our own sense of abundance is often derived from a highly individual and frequently unconscious set of values learned in our childhood and woven into the tapestry of our personal identity.

As a precursor to a deeper understanding of our overall relationship to abundance in its varied forms (as well as our ability to receive it), let's take a look at our relationship with money—one of the most powerful and generally misunderstood channels of abundance.

- What is your definition of money as it plays a role in your life?

- What are your first memories about money? Who passed down to you your family's stories and rules about money? What did you observe about having it and about not having it?

- What beliefs did you form about money early in your life, and how do those beliefs continue to govern your life today?

- How comfortable are you with the money you have in your life? Do you feel entitled to it? Obligated to share it or give it away? Is it a source of shame or guilt?

- In your pursuit of money, how often do you experience feelings of greed? Jealousy?

With bated breath …

Meditation: Passage into the Garden

Visualize yourself walking along a garden wall. It is deep spring, and the flowers are lush and fragrant. The wall twists and turns as it runs along the border of an extensive garden, replete with flowering shrubs and fruit trees in full blossom. Insects are busily pollinating, and birdsong fills the air.

As you make your way along the smooth stones of the path, you suddenly come to a hidden corner in the wall. And there, concealed in shadow, covered almost completely in dense, blooming vines, is a gate. Drawn to it, and possessed of a sudden and intense desire to see what is on the other side of the gate, you place your hand on its latch and press down.

You find yourself in a place of filtered light, neither inside nor outside the gate but rather a holding place, as if suspended in time. Before your eyes, you see the continuum of your life, the choices you made, your successes and the disappointments … all the steps of your journey that brought you here. Take the time to observe it fully. Then bless it all. As you step over the threshold, feel the past slipping away from you, completely released into the ethers.

Opening your etheric eyes, you find yourself in the main garden. Notice the beautiful colors, the music, the warm breezes and sounds of waves, the rustling of trees, exotic aromas of spices and blossoms. It is exquisitely beautiful here, and you feel completely at ease. In the distance, you see a group of lovely women. They are laughing and affectionate with one another—so free and easy. They are sitting, relaxed on the soft ground, with a radiant aura of light surrounding each of them. Just watching, you feel overcome by feelings of joy and gratitude and realize a longing to belong, to be a part of their group.

You allow yourself to drift closer to their circle, but as you approach, it begins to flicker and fade as if it were slipping into another frequency. You can barely hear their voices any longer. Disappointed, you start to turn away when one of the women glances up and gazes directly into your eyes. Reaching out her hand, she beckons to you, drawing you across the etheric boundary and into the sisterhood.

She leads you to an available spot on the ground, and taking your place, you exhale deeply. You find yourself feeling a great sense of relief. It is good to be here, and you realize you do belong. This is family. You realize that you have returned once again to this sacred place beyond space and time, that the sisterhood exists outside the limitations of the physical world. And that you are a part of this group—you always have been. And you understand that to belong, you have only to open your heart and remember.

Feeling centered and grounded and very connected, you intentionally begin the process of bringing yourself back to your ordinary reality. Breathing slowly and deeply, become aware of your physical body waiting quietly in your room. Gently open your eyes to the candlelight dancing next to you and sense the sisterhood gathered around you.

This evening, let's prepare to offer our gratitude, share our breakthroughs, and reveal what we have discovered about how we relate to money.

Closing Quote: We Stand at the Threshold
(Lisa Kagan excerpt from *We'Moon* 2011)

> We stand at the threshold
> learning how to be hard and soft at the same time,
> how to hold ourselves
> and still keep our arms open ...[58]

---

[58] Reproduced with permission from Lisa Kagan, excerpt from "We Stand at the Threshold," poem from *We'Moon Calendar Datebook 2011* (Wolf Creek, OR: Mother Tongue Ink, 2011).

Week 41

Inquiry: The Money Triggers

Before venturing further into our quest to embrace abundance, financial and otherwise, let's revisit the money quagmire to see what more we can excavate. The idea is to bring to the surface even more of our underlying beliefs, fears, and assumptions about money that we unconsciously carry around with us. By recognizing the triggers that activate our defensive and protective patterns, we can desensitize the issue of money and ultimately learn to deal with it as effectively as any other life dynamic.

In addition to last week's questions, consider these queries:

- When the going gets tough and the money runs thin, do you tighten your belt, or do you look for more income?

- Have you ever written down how much income you earn and from where? And how much money you spend and on what? The difference between the two is your *sustainability* (your profit or your loss). What does your sustainability look like?

- What are the words you hear in your head when you remember what your parent(s) told you about money? About work? About debt? About your own personal worth?

- How do you use your credit card—to float funds for a month (i.e., you pay it off in full each month), or as a long-term loan (i.e., to purchase things you can't afford now, for which you don't have the funds, nor a strategy to acquire them)?

- Is your discomfiture with money? Or rather with the *things* you want to purchase with the money?

- What meaning does this statement have for you: "Money helps us to help others as we help ourselves. Money might be called a catalyst for the Golden Rule. A sound and simple monetary system is probably the greatest material tool available to humanity for the multiplication of human satisfactions." [59] (Percy Greaves, Mises Institute of Economics)

Looking forward …

Meditation: The First Money Chakra

Make your personal space comfortable for the evening. … Light a candle, perhaps some incense. Close your eyes and settle in, relaxing into the soft, dark silence just behind your eyelids, and listen to the sound of my voice. Begin equalized breathing, drawing your breath gently in and then exhaling for approximately the same length of time. Make your breath slow and even. (Pause.)

Visualize yourself sitting on a large ball the color of deep red wine. The color itself is sensuous and exquisite, sparkling with nuances of blues and purples. It is very comfortable and easy to sit on this ball, and you find yourself sinking deeper and deeper into its surface. And as you sit, you notice its deep red colors seeping into the atmosphere surrounding you, tinting the air and your body with a rosy hue. Using your equalized breathing, begin to draw the glowing rose-colored light up through your roots, allowing it to illuminate the vast spaces of your first chakra. As the light illuminates your chakra, take a look around. Notice the massive root system securely connecting you to the planet below, channeling the earth's energies up through your roots, bringing sustenance to all your chakras above. Notice how sturdy and healthy your roots are, overflowing with an abundance of life force that continually fills your base chakra, like an underground spring.

Adjust your inner eye so you can actually *see* a spring, a beautiful pool in the very center of your first chakra, bubbling and

---

[59] Percy Greaves, Mises Institute of Economics (Auburn, AL, 1973).

overflowing with an infinite flow of incoming water light. Relax and notice how safe and protected you feel here.

Resting in this warm and rose-colored space, allow your mind and heart to relax and open.

I am now going to slowly list ten words. I want you to be attentive to what you see or hear in your mind's eye—any feelings, thoughts, or memories in response to each word. When you have identified your response or responses to each word, gently take them to the pool that sits in the middle of your base chakra and submerge them beneath the surface of the water light.

1) Poverty (Pause.)
2) Entitlement (Pause.)
3) Credit (Pause.)
4) Asset (Pause.)
5) Budget (Pause.)
6) Profit (Pause.)
7) Debt (Pause.)
8) Miserly (Pause.)
9) Afford (Pause.)
10) Extravagant (Pause.)

Allow all your responses to float in the pool, bouncing around in the bubbling red water light, being scrubbed clean. And when you can begin to see that they are no longer sticky with old stories and connotations, pick them up, dry them off, and drawing them through a full spectrum rainbow of colors, allow them to find a place in your heart. These ideas and pictures have no power over you. They are simply concepts that have been trapped in the confines of outdated beliefs and old memories. Without their baggage, you are free to live unencumbered in a world of infinite flow. And you are worthy of receiving it. Breathe in this message of freedom and self-esteem. Make it integral to your foundation.

Sensing it is time to return, feel the sangria-colored ball begin to deflate as it shrinks into a tiny point of light and disappears, leaving you floating effortlessly back to the ground where you find yourself once again in your candlelit room. In the center of the room is a group of beautiful women sitting rooted in a circle of radiance and power. There is a faint ruby glow to their countenances as they look up and motion for to you to join them. Gratefully, you do. Welcome back.

131

Closing Quotes: Two Money Quotes
(from Johann Wolfgang von Goethe and Ayn Rand)

Many people take no care of their money til they come nearly to the end of it,
and others do just the same with their time. [60] (Johann Wolfgang von Goethe)

Money is only a tool. It will take you wherever you wish, but it will not replace you as the driver. [61] (Ayn Rand)

---

[60] Johann Wolfgang von Goethe quote, public domain.
[61] Ayn Rand quote.

Week 41 Addendum

Additional Thoughts on Money Triggers

Several years back, I was asked to put together a course for Safe House about money. The women served by Safe House are mostly single moms, many of them illegal immigrants raising families under the radar, often on a cash-only basis. I called the course "It's Only Money, Honey" because I believe dealing with money needs to be demystified and made natural, like any other life dynamic.

In preparation for the course, I researched some history and theories of money. I also interviewed thirty people of diverse socioeconomic backgrounds to hear their beliefs, perceptions, and myths about money.

Here are some highlights of what I found:

About economics:

- It was regular people, not governments, who created money. It was created for the convenience of the common person.

- The commodity that is valued highest by the most people will become the most valuable and simplest medium of exchange. Eventually, in much of the world, this became metals—mostly gold, sometimes silver. Paper money is backed by these precious metals.

- Economics has its own immutable laws, and they cannot be regulated by governments, even though governments try. The regulations may create short-term effects, but in the long run, the laws of economics will prevail.

About human resources:

- It isn't the money that people actually want (with the exception of hoarders and coin collectors); it's what they believe the money can buy.

- After their basic needs are met, most people are not permanently motivated by money but rather by getting their emotional and social needs met. In business, this translates into the fact that, after basic needs are met, a raise does not increase the long-term morale of an employee as much as inclusion and recognition.

About religions:

- Most religions teach money is the root of evil and encourage redemption by giving the money to the religious organization. The Catholic Church has historically been one of the wealthiest entities on the globe.

From the general population:

- The attitudes and beliefs of your parents and elders toward money will directly impact your own attitudes and beliefs about money. This can also mean that if you carry unresolved issues with a significant person in your life, you will most likely carry unresolved issues with their beliefs and teachings, including about money.

- Objects, products, and experiences we were denied as children "because we can't afford it" become symbols of wealth and well-being when we are adults.

- This one is huge! If you hold a fixed level of money (abundance) in your mind/gut that you believe is appropriate for you, *you will not rise above that ceiling. If you do find yourself with significantly more than that amount, *you will spend it, lose it, or otherwise reduce your holdings until you are at or below the level you believe is appropriate for you.*

Examples of some family rules about money:

- A job is work. If work were fun, they wouldn't have to pay you to do it. So don't expect to enjoy your job.

- Value your own hard work. If something is given to you, you will not value it as much as if you had worked for it and earned it yourself.

- Always carry your own weight, pay your own share. No one likes a freeloader.

- Make your money ethically. If you make it any other way, the money is tainted, and whatever you buy with it is also tainted.

- Live within your means. Always know your place.

Week 42

Inquiry: Self-Worth and Money

Our next round in the imbroglio surrounding money … take a look at yourself through the lens of these queries:

- Are your business or professional fees *at or above* the mean for your industry?

- Do you provide yourself with the best equipment, the finest supplies, the optimal facility for your work?

- How confident are you in asking for someone to pay for your services? To pay their share? How comfortable are you borrowing from or loaning money to others?

- What is your biggest pet peeve regarding other people's behavior around money? What does that reflect about you?

- In considering one of your favorite abundance stories, what role did you play in making it happen?

Meditation: Honoring Our Root Chakra

Place yourself in a comfortable position. Inhaling and exhaling completely, breathe yourself into a place of calm and centeredness. … Release all the thoughts and concerns from your day and allow yourself to relax completely into this moment.

Bring your attention to your spine. Feel the powerful pulse of energy flowing up and down the entire length of your spine like an electric current. Breathing deeply, begin to draw this light energy down to the base of your spine, allowing it to collect in a luminous pool until it begins overflowing. See the light fill your whole root chakra, spiraling round and round in great clockwise circles, and watch your root chakra expand to accommodate the light now pouring into it, sweeping the whole energy field clean. When the chakra has been fully illuminated, allow the light energy to exit the base of your spine, channeling itself down and into the earth for renewal, carrying whatever toxins and negative energies have been released from your root chakra. Focus on remaining relaxed and open as the light continues to flow into and out of your root chakra and down into the earth to be neutralized.

As you watch it go, visualize this shaft of your body's light energy merging with the brilliant spectrum of radiant light that resides at the core of our planet, becoming a lifeline to your body above. Allow yourself to float, securely fastened to Mother Earth by this umbilical cord of light energy.

As this lifeline stretches from your body to the earth, notice there is now a second channel of energy, this one moving up toward you, as the earth's pure life force is now being transmitted back to you.

Feel the earth's energy flow up your roots and enter the base of your spine … bringing with it clean and pure energy, empowering and balancing your root chakra. Your root chakra is the energy center governing your physical body. A healthy root chakra promotes your physical well-being, your ability to meet your primary needs, and moves you from a state of fear and scarcity to a foundation of personal abundance.

Notice a subtle shift of your own life force as your root chakra clears, creating a sense of groundedness and intimate connection with the earth. Slowly open your etheric eyes and see the beautiful crimson color of your root chakra as it spins effortlessly in its clockwise rotation.

Inhaling and exhaling, allow more and more light to flow down from your body to the earth to be cleansed, and back up from the earth into the base of your spine. With each breath feel the empowerment, the resilience, and clarity generated by this light.

Continuing to breathe easily, feel your base chakra recalibrate as it brings a wonderful new sense of balance to your whole being.

Linda Laws

Remain open to any messages you may receive from the earth or from your root chakra during this time.

As you begin the process of return, remember to thank the earth light and thank yourself. With the memory of the beautiful, saturated red color of your root chakra still in your mind, begin your transition back to ordinary time and space, back to your own room with its candlelight flickering. … Settle yourself and open your eyes. Welcome back.

Closing Quote: Power
(J. Ruth Gendler from *The Book of Qualities*)

> Power made me a coat. For a long time I kept it in the back of my closet. I didn't like to wear it much, but I always took good care of it. When I first started wearing it again, it smelled like mothballs. As I wore it more, it started fitting better, and stopped smelling like mothballs.
>
> I was afraid if I wore the coat too much someone would want to take it, or else I would accidentally leave it behind in the *dojo* dressing room. But it has my name on the label now, and it doesn't really fit anyone else. When people ask me where I found such a becoming garment, I tell them about the tailor, Power, who knows how to make coats that you grow into. First, you must find the courage to approach Power and request a coat. Then, you must find the patience inside yourself to wear the coat until it fits. [62]

---

[62] Reproduced with permission of J. Ruth Gendler, "Power," from *The Book of Qualities* (New York, NY: Harper Perennial, 1988) ©1988 by J. Ruth Gendler.

Week 43

Inquiry: Abundance

And now, this week's topic is abundance. What is abundance?

Can you identify what makes your life feel abundant to you? Is it time? Options? Independence? Money? Influence? Friends?

What area(s) of your life would you characterize as most scarce? What is your belief about how they became that way?

What, specifically, are you willing to do to transform those scarce spaces into abundant spaces?

When?

Meditation: Temple of Prosperity

Settle yourself in a comfortable position and allow your body to relax into a state of openness and receptivity. Close your eyes and breathe. (Pause.) Gently place two fingers of one hand near your nose so that you can easily reach both nostrils with a minimum of movement. Begin by using one finger to close your left nostril. Slowly inhale deeply through the right nostril, bringing the air to the crown of your head. Then using your finger to close your right nostril, exhale your breath out your left nostril and pause. Now, breathe back in through your left nostril again up to your crown, pausing, and using your finger to close the left nostril, exhale out through the right. This is one full cycle of alternate nostril breathing. We will be breathing seven full cycles. As you breathe, you may find your breath becoming slower and deeper.

Your pauses may grow longer. Allow your own natural rhythm to guide you.

I will lead you through the first of the seven cycles. Then you will complete the remaining six cycles on your own. Ready? Using your finger, close your left nostril, slowly inhaling through the right nostril up to your crown, and hold. Then, close your right nostril and exhale out through the left. Pause. Inhale back in through the left again up to your crown, hold, and closing your left nostril, exhale out through the right. Okay, now you are on your own for six more rounds. (Pause.)

When you have completed all seven, lay your hands at your sides and allow a sense of peace to wash over you. Breathe slowly and evenly, and do not rush. (Long pause.)

As you open your etheric eyes, you find yourself standing in front of an ancient staircase that spirals far up into the distant heavens. Peering up, you see that the steps lead to a magnificent temple shimmering between several dimensions high above you. All around you, lush gardens extend as far as you can see, covering the land with an abundance of exquisite blossoms and lush vines. Balmy breezes whisper all around you and lazily caress your skin. The air is laden with the exotic scent of flowers and spices, alive with birdsong, insect buzzing and iridescent wings.

As you take in this supranatural scene, intoxicating music drifts down from above, melodies so moving, so unspeakably beautiful that they soar directly into your heart chakra … and open your heart. Immediately you are flooded with overflowing wonder and gratitude for the miracle of life and the unlimited possibilities available to you.

The music now begins to draw you forward, and, acquiescing, you ascend the ethereal stairwell going step by step into the indigo sky until you arrive in a vestibule with a gilded door which stands ajar. Glancing back and down, you see yourself still standing in the enchanted garden below, serenaded by music and songbirds. Reassured, you turn and push the door open and step over the threshold.

The chamber before you glows with otherworldly, radiant light, bursting with creative life force. You can sense the energetic charge pulsing the air. But there is absolutely nothing in the vastness of the chamber to be seen. As you gaze into the boundless emptiness, you suddenly comprehend that *the emptiness is not nothing; it is pregnant with everything. ... All the possibilities, all the seeds of infinite potential exist within the nothingness.* (Pause.)

Without warning, the temple chamber comes alive, and you find yourself drawn into the powerful and mysterious dance of creation. And as you dance, you begin to comprehend the seminal power of intention in the creation of all things. You suddenly understand*: intent is the key.* And *you must provide the intent* for your own creations. (Pause.) Setting aside any remaining reservations, you surrender yourself to the seduction of the dance, opening your heart and listening to its desires, for it is the heart's longings that give birth to the seeds of intention.

Eventually, the frenzy of the dance slows, the chamber once again recedes into a pregnant glow, and you are gently brought back to the enchanted garden in which your form still lingers amid the aromatic breezes. Held securely in your mind's eye lies the key to creation: your intent.

With great affection, you prepare yourself to reenter your physical body, patiently allowing your expanded self to be fully accommodated. And when you are centered and grounded once again, slowly open your eyes. Welcome back.

Closing Quote: Nothing Is Meant to Be
(Mike Dooley excerpt from tut.com)

> It's so tempting to look at your present life situation—who you're with, where you work, what you have and have not—and think to yourself: "This was obviously meant to be ... I'm here for a reason."

> And to a degree, you'd be right. BUT, you "are where you are" because of the thoughts you *used to* think, and *may still* think;

> And so, you "are where you are" to learn: "*This is how life works*"—NOT because "*it was meant to be.*"

Don't give away your power to vague or mysterious logic. Tomorrow is a blank slate in terms of people, work and play, because it, too, will be of your making. And you will again have that sense that it was "meant to be," no matter who or what you've drawn into your life.

Nothing is *"meant to be"* except for your *freedom to choose and your power to create.*

Choose big and be happy. The Universe[63]

---

[63] Reproduced with permission from Mike Dooley, from *The Universe Talks*, © www.tut.com.

Week 44

Inquiry: Being Able to Receive

In a natural progression of our quests over the last several weeks concerning abundance and its many forms and implications, this week we ask the pivotal question: are you willing and able to receive?

Take a peek at the questions below and let's see how we fare:

- When was the last time you spent a generous amount of *time* doing exactly what *you* wanted to do? What was it?

- When was the last time you spent a significantly generous amount of *money* on something that was extraordinary, *just for you* (i.e., not for the household, not something economical or practical)? What was it?

- When you *do* attract abundance to you, how comfortable are you with it? Do you feel the urge to hide it, share it, give it away? Do you downplay your desire for it, your role in acquiring it, your worthiness to enjoy it?

- When you acquire something long desired, do you secretly fear the price you will have to pay—socially? psychologically? financially?

Whew! It's getting bright in here!

Meditation: Loving Yourself Meditation

Take a moment to light a candle if you wish. Find a comfortable position, sitting or lying back, and visualize yourself in a peaceful water setting—a river, a lake, the ocean, a geothermal pool—whatever you find restful. Close your eyes and allow yourself to sink into the water to a comfortable depth, whatever that level is. When you find yourself there, simply stop sinking … and allow yourself to float effortlessly, the water buoying you up, massaging your muscles and gently caressing your skin in its silken currents.

Relax into the water as it draws out the tension carried in your physical form, dissolving and transmuting it.

Slowly, using your etheric hands, bring your pointer finger to your thumb, forming a ring. Allow your hand to gently fall open with your palm facing up and away from you. This is called the Cin Mudra, the ultimate symbol for creating peace and loving kindness around you. This mudra connects directly into your heart chakra and channels the energy of giving and receiving love. This evening, we will use the Cin Mudra to call these energies to ourselves.

Bringing your attention to your breath, notice how it falls into its own natural rhythm, gently breathing in, holding, easily breathing out … endlessly bringing in the life force energy, recharging the energetic field surrounding your body.

In this state of deep peace and receptivity, visualize these thoughts lying in the palm of your hand and slowly bring them into your heart:

> *I am good enough exactly as I am.* (Pause.)
> *I am worthy of the very best.* (Pause.)
> *I am the creator of all my thoughts.* (Pause.)
> *There is more than enough available for all of us.*
> (Pause.)

Sense the infinity of love in which you exist, the energy that flows from the heart of life itself in such great supply. Feel yourself open to this unconditional source of abundance, continuing to breathe easily, in and out, as you expand into it. Feel the collective life force as it pulsates in and around you like a heartbeat. Allow yourself to rest in the spaces between your incoming and outgoing breath, receiving, assimilating, integrating. Enjoy the tremendous spaciousness of it. (Pause.)

And now, remaining mindful of your newly expanded state, prepare for your return to ordinary consciousness. Rising from the water, dry yourself off and make your way back to your room, settling yourself once again in the circle of women who are delighted to see you. Breathing fully and easily … when you are ready, open your eyes. Welcome back.

Closing Quote: My Symphony
(William Henry Channing)

To live content with small means,
To seek elegance rather than luxury,
And refinement rather than fashion,
To be worthy, not respectable, and wealthy, not rich,
To study hard, think quietly, talk gently, act frankly,
To listen to stars and birds, babes and sages, with open heart,
To bear all cheerfully,
Do all bravely,
Await occasions,
Hurry never—
In a word, to let the spiritual, unbidden and unconscious, grow up though the common.
This is to be my symphony.[64]

---

[64] William Henry Channing poem, public domain.

∽

Week 45

Inquiry: A Night of Impromptu

This week, let's lighten up—nothing to read, no preparation—playtime! Bring your child.

Meditation: Embrace Your Bliss
(Leena St. Michael, "Embrace Your Bliss," for the March 8, 2016 International Women's Day in NYC, adapted for time)

The United Nation's International Women's Day provides a time for global reflection on progress made, to call for change and to celebrate acts of courage and determination by ordinary women who have played extraordinary roles in the history of our countries and our communities.

The 2016 theme for International Women's Day was "Planet 50-50 by 2030: Step it Up for Gender Equality." The United Nations asks us to envision reaching this goal *before* 2030.

Let's settle into a comfortable position, close your eyes, and take three full breaths. Open your mind's eye to the not so radical vision of a world of *Gender Equality and Empowerment,* and *Equal Rights for all Women and Girls.*

As I relate to you the points of the United Nations initiative, use your breath to draw each visualization into your energy field, holding it there as reality.

There are five:

- All girls and boys, worldwide, have access to quality Early Childhood Development, Early Childhood Care, and Pre-Primary Education so that they are ready for Primary Education. (Breathe.)
- All girls and boys complete free, equitable and quality Primary and Secondary Education, leading to effective learning outcomes. (Breathe.)
- All forms of Discrimination Against All Women and Girls, everywhere, are *dissolved*. (Breathe.)
- All forms of Violence Against All Women and Girls, *in the public and private spheres*, including trafficking and all forms of exploitation, are *eradicated*. (Breathe.)
- Child marriage, early and forced marriage, and female genital mutilation are *abolished*. (Breathe.)

Let us breathe gratitude for the achievements of Every Woman: our Mothers, our Grandmothers, our Daughters, female business owners, health professionals, volunteers, political leaders and teachers—any mentors anywhere who come to mind—and for all of us who have transcended limiting concepts and have expanded our potential, not only as women, but as human beings.

Let us celebrate the nurturing aspects of men, and the many men and boys who lift up women and honor them. (HeForShe is one organization which enlists the commitment of men and boys.)

AND, let us each continue to envision, and work with grace, with women locally and globally, to achieve the UN goals for the world. And together, let us continue to serve the greater good with The Power of Universal Womanhood. [65]

---

[65] Leena St. Michael, adapted from "Embrace Your Bliss" for the March 8, 2016 International Women's Day in New York City, NY.

With a deep exhale, release it all and bless it all. ... Amen ... so mote it be.

And now, gently bring yourself back to your body, back to your room, to your consciousness of the beautiful, intentional, and revolutionary women sitting around our circle tonight. ... Welcome back, Evolutionaries! There is a phenomenon known as the butterfly effect, whereby a small change in one system can have large effects somewhere else. In other words, a butterfly flapping its wings in Rio de Janeiro might just shift the weather in Baltimore. I think we are doing our share of flapping.

Playtime Topics: This evening, whoever would like to go first, please announce yourself. I will then randomly select one of the ten topics already written on folded pieces of paper:

1. When did you first realize you were part animal/bird/ reptile/insect? What function does that part play in your life?

2. Have you ever been, by your own criteria, outrageous in public? What did you learn?

3. If you could invite any three people in history or literature to dinner, who would you invite and why?

4. What would your father say is your best trait? Your worst? How has that influenced how you've lived your life so far?

5. What fantasy, in film or literature, are you most attracted to? What is so appealing about it?

6. What benefit did you first realize when you began operating outside of the expected norm? How did that alter your course? What have been the disadvantages?

7. What is the best advice you've ever received? What is the best advice you've ever given?

8. What is your earliest memory, and how has it been significant to you over your lifetime?

9. When did you realize your parents were people? How did that change who you thought they were?

10. Why did you wait so long? What have been the benefits, the penalties?

Closing Quote: Don't Sit Still
(Renee Hummel ©2006)

Don't sit still!
Let your inner being pulse with the wings of a bird
rising and falling with the breath.
Let the wild thing inside you soar beyond its cage
unseen by the keepers of the classroom or the office
who would have you stay motionless,
dying within your skin.

Don't sit still!
as though your teeming energy submitted to these
chains.
Let the waters of your body roar,
churning oceans in a seashell.
Let the rhythmic snake inside climb the tree unseen.
Let the tips of your fingers open, curiously,
each one the eye of some wild creature.

Don't sit still!
Let your inner being venture out into the wildest
terrain,
tasting the fruits that flourish there,
tasting the fresh unsheltered sky.
Deftly seek the motion that you may find in stillness,
for there is a current of life inside you, strong
enough to lift
your pinioned feathers into flight.[66]

---

[66] Reproduced with permission of Renee Hummel, "Don't Sit Still," ©2006 Renee Hummel, dreneehummel@gmail.com. Renée lives in Colorado and loves to share poetry that uplifts and inspires.

Week 46

Inquiry: Running Our Number

The quandary that remains with us always is, how do we see our way forward *while we are standing in our way?*

Whatever path we are following, whatever game we are playing, if we have not made the progress intended, if we discover we have veered off course onto some tangent, we are being presented with an opportunity to *see the game we have, in reality, chosen to play instead.*

If we are honest with ourselves, we can see ourselves running our number: the strategies we use to deal with uncomfortable or difficult situations while not addressing them directly, our efforts to reduce our anxiety while maintaining our self-image at the same time.

The question is, do we want to break through it?

Take a look. Write a list of three reasons you originally embarked on a particular, significant course of action. Now, compare those initial reasons to the three top reasons you haven't successfully arrived yet. What do you see?

Meditation: Silence Meditation
(adapted from Tripurashakti.com, Yoga Meditation)

Allow yourself to settle, wherever you are. Take some time to light a candle and perhaps some pleasing incense to clear the area around you. Allow your attention to move inward, taking the senses along with your focus to that innermost silent space …

moving down through the surface layers of your being and finally allowing your attention to come to rest where your own pure consciousness resides. No matter how shallow or deep you dive, as soon as you leave the noise of the surface behind you can begin to enjoy the Silence.

Pause here for a moment, breathing slowly and evenly, enjoying the stillness and clarity. Your space may be private to you or you may share a communal silent space with other beings—your guides, the grandmothers—all part of the oneness ….

Allow the layers of "who you are not" … all the masks and beliefs—your body, your mind, your physical senses—allow them to drift to the side as you enjoy being in the center of this still pool of quiet. (Pause.)

As you are drawn more deeply inward, surrender to the sense of profound calm that begins to permeate your whole being. (Pause.)

Consider how it might feel to make this Silence the platform from which you live, the freedom of being able to choose, consciously, when you wish to wear the layers of "not you," and when you wish to take them off … the possibility of fully participating in the waking state *while your awareness remains resting in the Silence.*

If you lose the Silence during the busy-ness of your day, you can simply recede back into your Self, bringing your attention back to that place where the Silence lives and begin perceiving life from that stillness again, looking out through all the layers of what is not really you, until you transition … and once again become pure, naked consciousness.

Mastering these transition moments allows us to be active in the outer world while not falling asleep in it. (Pause.) [67]

Now, gradually bring your awareness back to your body. Begin to modulate your breathing until your natural breath returns. Take a few seconds to orient, and when you feel centered and grounded, draw yourself back up and into the light of this reality. Open your eyes and leap into the present moment! Welcome back.

---

[67] "Silence Meditation," adapted from *Yoga Meditation*, Tripurashakti.com.

This evening, our inquiry asks us to look at when we get lured off our track by believing our own sleight of hand. Who would like to begin by sharing their gratitudes and breakthroughs? I'm tossing the talking stick into the center of our circle now.

Closing Quote: Setting a Cup for Shadow
(Rain Crowe 2012, from *We'Moon 2014*)

> When coming to circle, sisters check in by saying a few words of what energy each is holding as they come to the gathering, their gratitudes, and so forth …
>
> A cup of water is set on the table for Shadow, by which that stealthy entity may be checked in, and the invisible given visibility. To be clear, Shadow is not *invoked*, it is simply acknowledged as already being in the room. It is the neglected or repressed parts of our being, which are both our essential, consistent places of struggle, *and* our magnificent, un-ripened, un-picked potential.
>
> We can ignore these parts, to our detriment, for then, their presence moves only through the cracks given, unintentionally, as we inter-relate without full consciousness. Seeping or banging their way into the room with exaggerated visibility, they can hold us hostage at inconvenient or painful moments. Or, we can set a cup for the Shadow parts of ourselves and our groups, to honor them as maps for how to heal, step into our power, and live well in these times.
>
> When Shadow presents in the room, we can look at the cup, be reminded to honor Shadow, and step towards vulnerability and compassion, with insight as our ally. We can become mirrors to ourselves and for each other, energizing prayers for releasing those patterns and creating new neural pathways in the minds of our beings and our togetherness.

Changing behaviors, changes the mind. Changing the mind, changes the Mind.

Changing the Mind, changes the World.

The Alchemy of Revolution is possible in each moment! [68]

---

[68] Reproduced with permission from Rain Crowe, "Setting a Cup for Shadow," from *We'Moon Calendar Datebook 2014* (Wolf Creek, OR: Mother Tongue Ink, 2014), ©2012 Rain Crowe.

❦

Week 47

Inquiry: An Act of Recovery

Continuing upon your life's path with your bag of old tools, tricks, and treasures slung over your shoulder, sooner or later it may come to your attention there is a hole in your bag! As you look back, you notice some of your treasures lying abandoned along the pathway, lost identities, discarded personas, old behaviors, even faded interests.

Allow yourself the time to go back and reexamine what you have intentionally or inadvertently left behind, to make peace with what you choose to leave discarded and to recognize and reclaim that which could be of renewed value to you now. Our sense of integration and wholeness fluctuates as we shift and evolve on our life's journey. And yet throughout those changes and spurts of growth, our authentic selves continue to reflect our core essence if we can remain alert.

Come prepared to share your process of remembering yourself. What gems have you found?

What dross have you relinquished for good?

Meditation: Moving to Wholeness

Take three slow breaths, inhaling and exhaling. ... Allow your mind to shift into neutral. ... Release the day and feel your body begin to slip into theta as you envision yourself far above the planet. See the multitudes of stars and distant planets that coexist with us in the heavens.

Below you, hanging suspended in the silent blackness, is our beautiful earth with her blue waters and green land masses, rotating and revolving faithfully in her place in the galaxy like a shining jewel.

In your mind's eye, see the earth's inhabitants, all its creatures and the nature kingdom, living in a state of natural beauty, surrounded by music, drenched in a zillion colors … all so similar, all caring for their beloveds. Allow your heart to feel the implicit love that has made this universe possible.

As the merchants, scientists, and technologists collaborate to make our world smaller and smaller, see too the tremendous opportunities for compassion and cooperation across countless boundaries, the undiluted potential for creating universal harmony and integration among all living beings, for bridging the gaps between science and art, doctrines and philosophies, the fortunate and less fortunate, the genders and generations.

Watching the earth spinning perfectly beneath you, become aware now of a second, closer aspect of this integration … *personal integration* … an integration that enables you to participate not only in global harmony but also in *a meaningful integrated way within your own being … in your own life.*

What would be the *next best step* for you to move toward your own personal integration within the whole, to reclaim your natural state as part of the oneness? Envision the lost or discarded parts of yourself as they too float in the black and silent space around you. They may appear in the form of images or words, old dreams or activities that were once a part of the self you are seeking to reclaim. Allow them to come to you now for review. (Pause.)

As you embrace your own many aspects, choose those you wish to retain and allow those that no longer fit to be fully released. Feel your energy become more aligned into the pattern that is your genuine self—your own tempo, your own palette. (Pause.)

And know that as you restore your own being to its natural balance in its innate state of equilibrium, so too your family, your culture, our entire planet will become more purely aligned with their essences as well.

We are holistic beings, an integral part of the whole. As we integrate ourselves, we heal the oneness of which we are a part. This is our magic, our power as human beings.

Begin to bring your more integrated self back now, rejoining with that blue and green jewel we call our home, mystic riders together on the planet Earth. As you reenter your body, gently adjust the fit until you are comfortable once again and allow your own natural breath to return. Welcome back.

Closing Quote: More Than We Know
(Rachel Naomi Remen, excerpt from Living Fully.com)

> We are all more than we know.
> Wholeness is never lost, it is only forgotten.
>
> Integrity *rarely* means that we need to *add* something to ourselves; it is more an *un*doing than a doing, a freeing of ourselves from beliefs we have—about who we are, about the ways we have been persuaded to "fix" ourselves to know who we genuinely are.
>
> Even after many years of seeking, thinking and living one way, we are able to reach past all that to claim our integrity, to embrace our genuine self, and to live in a way we may never have expected to live. [69]

---

[69] Rachel Naomi Remen, excerpt from LivingFully.com.

Week 48

Inquiry: The Nuances of Possessions

This week, let's consider some of the more subtle nuances of physical possessions.

Some of us have no difficulty attracting or manifesting in the physical realm but cannot for the life of us retain it. Our treasures slip away, ebb away, or lose their appeal … leaving us disappointed and feeling empty, exactly the opposite of what we had hoped.

Some of us acquire physical possessions and then hold on to them past their time of usefulness. Our possessions ultimately become burdens that drain our psychic energy, crowd our physical space, and preoccupy our minds.

And still others of us remain in a perpetual state of scarcity, seemingly unable to manifest on any plane … physical, mental, emotional, or spiritual.

I think we have all experienced these states of being at one time or another. What insights can you share about how you were able to navigate these challenges? What did you do to shift them?

Meditation: Choosing Openness

Allow your eyes to close. Relax your entire body by breathing deeply three times, each time exhaling completely. Let go of the day. … Gently liberate all thoughts and thought forms that may be attached to you and allow the space surrounding you to be clear and empty … *open space*. Breathe in the openness; breathe in the possibilities that exist there. ... Notice what color the openness is for you.

As you continue to breathe deeply, begin to use your breath to gently massage your forehead and temples, the crown of your head, and down your neck. Breathe into each bone and muscle, each sinew and synapse, and allow your breath to relax and loosen the skeletal structure just enough to infuse all the in-between spaces with your sacred breath. Keep it easy and loose, breathing gently. Allow the color of openness to permeate your inner spaces ... (Pause.)

Slowly move your breath down your body into your chest cavity, opening the spaces there, moving the breath in and bringing color to your heart. Breathe into your arms and fingers, relaxing and expanding their physical forms, and now down into the abdomen. Allow all your organs to rest in the spaciousness that surrounds them. ... Feel your blood moving easily throughout the vessels of your body. Inhale deeply and allow the color of your openness to fill the center of your body and allow it to rest there, pulsating softly.

Now begin to move the breath down to the base of your spine. Feel your etheric roots expand and soften as they move even deeper into the earth, grounding and connecting you. And finally, breathe down your legs and into your feet, breathing color into each toe. As you exhale, feel the breath leave your body from the bottoms of your feet and the top of your head at the same time. Empty out. ... Relax into the capaciousness of your whole being.

Allow the color of your openness to flow into and throughout all your bodies—mental, physical, emotional, astral, etheric, and soul—bringing your awareness to the vast sense of peace and unboundedness you can now feel all around you. Completely surrender into this moment, into this simple place of choice, into this place of unattached openness.

From this state of infinite possibility, quietly affirm to yourself:

- *I am enough, exactly as I am.*

- *This state of spaciousness, flow and clarity is the place from which I derive my lifeblood.*

- *My own breath sustains me; the better I breathe, the more life energy I will have.*

- *My intrinsic, internal well-being is not determined by outside circumstances. Other people, places, events and beliefs systems do not define my choices.*

- *I will remember the color of my openness. This is my prana.*

And now, slowly allowing your own natural breath to return, begin guiding your body back from this short time away. Allow yourself to assimilate and integrate the openness you have just experienced. Notice how this state of being feels and resolve to make it your forever choice. Reemerging into normal space and time, take a moment to savor the feeling of joyous renewal and wholeness that now radiates from you.

Remember to breathe slowly and easily, empowering the universal energy to flow in and around your body. Ask your energy to continue to enliven you as you begin to make your way back to the circle and to our call this evening as we consider the subtleties of the physical realm. Who would like to be first this evening to take up the talking stick to share their gratitudes and breakthroughs?

Closing Quotes: Two Quotes on Possessions
(Russell W. Belk, Ram Dass)

> We cannot hope to understand consumer behavior without first gaining some understanding of the meanings that consumers attach to possessions. A key to understanding what possessions mean is recognizing that, knowingly or unknowingly, intentionally or unintentionally, we regard our possessions as parts of ourselves.[70] (Russell W. Belk)

> I resolved to keep lightening my game as much as I could. But when you have beautiful things that are a part of the beauty of your life, of

---

[70] Russell W. Belk, "Possessions and the Extended Self," excerpt from *Journal of Consumer Research*, September 1, 1988 (Chicago, IL: University of Chicago Press, 1988).

course, enjoy them. What happens is, as you keep becoming more light in your consciousness, you feel less desire to collect stuff. What you have already is part of the beauty of your universe.[71] (Ram Dass)

---

[71] Ram Dass, excerpt from *Here and Now Talks*, 1992.

Week 49

Inquiry: The Neutral Zone

Making the decision to move in a new direction may be initiated by the desire to move away from the old or toward the new, or both … but the first step is always into that place of transition—the space of no longer here but not yet there, the incredibly potent *neutral zone*.

The neutral zone can feel uncomfortable because we experience it as unproductive, as if we are making little progress. We may be tempted to rush through it to get to the next step in our process. Don't do it! It is in this neutral zone where we truly disengage from and digest our past. The digestion is important to being able to assimilate what we have learned; without it, we tend to simply recreate the old, perhaps in a slightly new or altered form.

Choose a change you are currently going through, or one that you are considering making, or one you remember from your past; share with us what you have learned about being in the neutral zone.

Meditation: Pre-Solstice Meditation

Begin by taking a few deep breaths, settling into your heart space. Allow your breath to be slow and even, inhaling and exhaling evenly and deeply.

Feel your body begin to relax. Notice that you are now in a beautiful and calm place deep inside yourself. Continue breathing into your heart chakra, inhaling golden light with each breath. As you fill up with this golden light, begin also bringing in uplifting thoughts, memories, and dreams and allow them to spiral round and round your heart chakra, absorbing the golden light. Bring in your intentions for forgiveness and peace, your intentions for love and for healing, and allow them too to become part of the spiral that pulsates with the light in your heart space. Notice that as you become lighter, your heart becomes more and more open. (Pause.)

And now envision your loved ones—those who are close and those who remain at a distance, those you know and those you do not know yet—and begin sending these light energies from your heart chakra out into the ethers … sharing your intentions for love, peace, and healing … beyond all boundaries and differences. Continue to breathe the light into and out of your heart chakra, balanced and rhythmic, allowing your intentions for the highest good to flow forth from you. Balance channeling the light in and the intentions out, until it feels easy and comfortable … like your own natural breath. (Pause.)

And now begin to direct the flow of these energies to your own self, allowing the flow to emit from your heart and to be absorbed back into your solar plexus, "the place where the sun's light enters." Be certain you are open and willing to receive these gifts of the light. (Pause.)

When you feel complete, begin to bring yourself back to what you have come to think of as your ordinary reality, slipping smoothly into your physical form, remembering to bring your light and your love as you rejoin the sisters who surround you this evening in our expanded circle.

This evening, on the eve of the solstice, our inquiry asks us to consider neutral space—the space in between here and there—a place of standstill. Fittingly, the word solstice means "to come to a stop, to stand still."

Closing Quote: Where the Light Enters
(Rumi)

> I said, "what about my eyes?"
> God said, "keep them on the road."
> I said, "what about my passion?"

God said, "keep it burning."
I said, "what about my heart?"
God said, "tell me what you hold inside it."
I said, "pain, sorrow, doubt."
God said, "Stay with it. The wound is the place
where the light enters you."[72]

---

[72] Rumi quote, public domain.

Week 50

Inquiry: Tending the Cauldron

Taking an extended look at the neutral zone … Wise Woman legend calls it "tending the cauldron."

Simply put, it is the solitary time we set aside for our own deepest healing—to feed the fire, adjust the spices, simmer the ingredients just so. We willingly commit to staying within our inner space, preparing the stew of our experience for digestion and assimilation. As we regain our clarity and strength, forward movement becomes possible again. We are able to hear our calling. It may come from internal guidance or from an outside source. In order to hear, one must come to know the interrelatedness of one's own mind, heart, and gut and be able to recognize when they are, all three, aligned with life's flow.

How brews your stew? Are you settling into the art of being passive with a purpose? Or have you found resistance, punctuated by the urge to push through?

Meditation: Colored Waterfalls Meditation

Let's start by taking several deep breaths. With each breath, feel yourself moving deeper and deeper into a state of peace and relaxation.

Now, notice in front of you an opening in the fabric of time. Stepping carefully through the portal, you begin to move one step at a time, through the channel until you have made your way to the other side … where you find yourself in the most heavenly valley, filled with flowers and trees, soft sunshine with a sky-blue

canopy above. Notice how much easier it is to breathe here. …
Feel the gentle, tingling sensation of your body expanding as
energy flows into you.

One side of the valley is bounded by a massive cliff covered
with huge boulders and towering trees, and you find yourself
approaching this vast wall of rock. Walking closer, you become
aware of hundreds of beautiful waterfalls tucked into the folds of
the flora, cascading down the face of the rock, pouring into deep
pools at the bottom. Each waterfall is vibrant with color, the water
saturated in its own unique hue, and each pool is surrounded by a
variety of mosses and blossoms that give off their own intoxicating
scent.

As you stand gazing at this spectacular cliff with its magnificent
waters, you spot one waterfall you find particularly attractive. You
feel inexplicably drawn to it … and you go. As you approach, the
mist of the falls swirls around you like a sweetly scented fog, lovingly
embracing you in its watery presence, leading you deeper into the
pool until you are standing directly under the water showering
down from above. You stand entranced as the water dances lightly
all around you, rhythmically caressing your hair, soothing your
shoulders, infusing your entire body with pure life force.

Allow any remaining tightness you carry to loosen, any depression
to lift. Feel the release of all anxiety, confusion, or blockages as
they are washed away like grime, into the pool. Become aware of
your feet resting gently on the soft bottom of the pool, grounding
you to the earth as you are filled with the pure effervescence of
water song.

Take the time to stand beneath the waters until you feel renewed.
(Pause.)

Although you may feel hesitant to leave this healing place, you
know it is now time to go. Turn one last time to watch the
wall of falling water, endlessly washing the mountain clean, like
rainbow–colored tears.

Gradually moving back into the now, become aware of your body
lying still and allow your own natural breath to return. Begin to
take note of your surroundings, and when you feel ready, move to
take your place again in the circle of women who call themselves
sisters of the light. Welcome back!

Linda Laws

Closing Quote: Tell Us of Pain
(Kahlil Gibran, excerpt from *The Prophet*)

And a woman spoke, saying, "Tell us of Pain."
And he said:
Your pain is the breaking of the shell that encloses your understanding.
Even as the stone of the fruit must break, that its heart may stand in the sun, so must you know pain.
And could you keep your heart in wonder at the daily miracles of your life, your pain would not seem less wondrous than your joy;
And you would accept the seasons of your heart, even as you have always accepted the seasons that pass over your fields.
And you would watch with serenity through the winters of your grief.
Much of your pain is self-chosen.
It is the bitter potion by which the physician within you heals your sick self.
Therefore, trust the physician, and drink his remedy in silence and tranquility;
For his hand, though heavy and hard, is guided by the tender hand of the Unseen,
And the cup he brings, though it burn your lips, has been fashioned of the clay which the Potter has moistened with His own sacred tears.[73]

---

[73] Kahlil Gibran, "Tell Us of Pain," excerpt from *The Prophet* (New York, NY: Alfred A. Knopf Publisher, 1923), public domain.

Week 51

Inquiry: The Art of Surrender

There is a lot to be said for the ability to surrender. Whether you have been brought to your knees by an uncompromising life situation or have learned to proactively flow with a life-changing event or circumstance, the capacity to surrender can alter not only your interior process but also the outcome.

We may surrender to change or to the death of a way of being. We may surrender to the restoration process of that which needs healing. Sometimes we must surrender to that which cannot ever be made whole and needs simply to be accepted as it is. Surrender's companion is compassion, and initially, compassion must be bestowed by and upon one's self.

What soul lessons have been entrusted to you while walking the footpaths of surrender? What were your challenges, and what were your successes? How willing are you now to invoke surrender as a preferred modus operandi in your earth walk?

Meditation: The Ledge

Envision yourself standing on the edge of a beautiful cliff looking out over the ocean. The setting sun is just sinking below the horizon and, in its final moments, casts its departing rays of light high into the sky, saturating the clouds in deep purples, magenta, yellow, and orange—brilliant against the darkening indigo heavens.

A gentle wind brushes your skin, swirling your hair about your head. Entranced, you stand above the panorama, mesmerized as distant waves break on the shore far below, the sound of the surf soft and rhythmic.

You consciously release the tension in your neck, your shoulders, and your back and relax your stance on the rock ledge, allowing the evening to bathe your body in sensation, drenching your senses with color and sound, all the while the soft, wet mist hangs suspended in the air around you.

Now, begin to feel the cliff upon which you are standing start to fall away. There is no longer a rocky ledge there. In its place, a buoyant, breathy cushion of compressed air presses up against the soles of your feet, invoking a weightlessness, strange but familiar, as if in a dream. You raise your arms up knowingly, and leaning out over the sand below, you drift out and up into the thermals, your arms open wide and strong, just the way you have always done. …

You may discover your natural movement is a slow and gentle drifting, or you may find yourself enjoying short, quick bursts that seem more like long leaps from place to place. You may prefer a high-velocity, soaring flight, swooping and spiraling through the sky. Whatever your place of comfort within this world of air and ether, you find it. And settling into your own space within it, you feel imbued with a new sense of freedom, unfettered and all the while protected.

Allow yourself to enjoy this state of lightness, gliding in the warmth far above the earth as you come to a new recognition of your own balance and center, derived not from the ground with which you are so accustomed … but from your inner compass. (Pause.)

Bringing your attention back to your body now, allow the sensations of passing air to slow … and finding a safe and familiar place on the land below, begin your descent, allowing the currents to ferry you safely back to the sacred space you call home. Notice how easy it is to land and to once again embody your earth self. Take a few deep breaths. Shake yourself off. Welcome back!

Closing Quotes: Butterfly Quotes
(Miss Ascentia from *We'Moon 2016*; Maya Angelou)

When a butterfly is ready to emerge from its chrysalis, it chews a tiny hole in one end and forces its stunning new form through the small orifice.

Within this struggle of emergence, liquids from deep inside the butterfly's body are secreted into the capillaries of its wings, where they harden to ensure the strength and capacity for the butterfly to fly and survive. When denied this struggle the butterfly dies. [74] (excerpt from Miss Ascentia)

We delight in the beauty of the butterfly, but rarely consider the changes it has gone through to achieve that beauty. [75] (Maya Angelou)

---

[74] Miss Ascentia quote from *We'Moon Calendar Datebook 2016* (Wolf Creek, OR: Mother Tongue Ink, 2016).

[75] Maya Angelou quote.

Week 52

Inquiry: Embracing the Who That We Are

Now that we have examined our circumstances from myriad viewpoints and over some extended period of time, and perhaps surrendered in some way to the idea that our life is offering up the opportunities and challenges that are perfectly coordinated with our soul's path, consider these queries:

- Can you embrace the *who* that you are, *exactly the way you are right now*, and gratefully celebrate the moment?

- Do you accept the perfection of yourself *without holding on to some future, improved version*?

- What might allow you to find comfort in, or an easy expansion into, *just being yourself*—with all your uniqueness and eccentricities?

Opening our arms …

Meditation: Soul Seeds

Settle yourself for tonight's call. You may wish to light a candle or some incense. Center yourself and take some deep cleansing breaths. … Relax, releasing all conscious thought and any tensions you may be carrying. Simply listen to the sound of my voice and envision a soft, diffused white light surrounding you … (Pause.)

In your mind's eye and from your heart's center, begin reciting this prayer: "I ask to know, and to have the humility and grace to receive and accept, the manifestations of my soul's intent for this lifetime. I ask for my own highest good and for the benefit of the whole."

Now, begin listening to your own higher self for the desires that come forth to be heard. You may need to listen deeply to a still, small voice … or you may be bowled over by a thunderous response. You may hear one overriding desire, or there may be a multitude of intentions clamoring to be heard. They may be interrelated or be widely diverse and unconnected.

Listen patiently and try to hear without judgment or censoring, without attempting to understand. … Simply absorb what you are hearing into your innermost core and know that it will take root there. (Pause.)

A new moon is a time to focus on *you* … not the small, myopic you … the expansive, available you whose authority and power flows effortlessly when you manifest and share your energy from your soul self.

It is important to learn how to do the right thing in alignment with the intentions of your own soul, and from this place of integrity, we can then become the catalyst for others to also be inspired to do their right thing.

Learn to be the source that channels your own soul's seeds of intentions. Learn to share your life force while maintaining your boundaries, and above all else, value and nourish your own spiritual well-being.

Tonight we are sowing spiritual seeds into the gardens of our lives. Lovingly wrap these sacred seeds of the soul in silver and golden light and allow them to migrate to the chakra with which they are most closely aligned, knowing that they will be held there safely to flourish in accordance with their own manifest destiny.

And now begin your return, shifting effortlessly back through the dimensions until you find yourself once again sitting in a circle with a group of luminous women. Take some time to settle yourself into your physical form, and taking a few earthly breaths, open your eyes. Welcome back.

Closing Quote: Gardening, a Form of Prayer
(Kaya McLaren, excerpt from *Church of the Dog*)

For me, gardening is a form of prayer. Most people have an awareness of Life and Death, but few have an awareness of Life, Death and Life Again. Gardeners do, though.

Bulbs come up every spring. Then, in winter, it looks like there's nothing there, no hope for life ever again. Then Hallelujah! Next spring they're back even fuller. It's the same thing with perennials.

Annuals have a slightly different lesson. Annuals really do die, but they broadcast seeds before they go. Where there was only one [Forget-Me-Not] the year before, there will be ten this year, and one day, they will fill every empty space in your garden. Annuals are a lesson in the difference one living thing—plant or person—can make and how its presence resonates long after it's gone.

The effects, of course, are not immediate. There is always the winter. And when you consider the garden as a whole, well, winter is a time to reflect—a time to dream. It gives you time to ask the big questions.

Gardening is an affirmation of divine timing.[76]

---

[76] Reproduced with permission of Penguin Publishing Group, Kaya McLaren, "Gardening is a Form of Prayer," from *Church of the Dog* (New York, NY: Penguin Books, an imprint of Penguin Publishing Group, a division of Penguin Random House LLC), pages 152–153, © 2000, 2008 Penguin Publishing Group. All rights reserved.

Bringing a Circle to Its Final Close

Closing a Circle—Step 1: Considering Bringing a Circle to a Close

After much soul searching and in consultation with the elder sisters, we have come to a decision to bring our circle itself to a resting place for thirty days. Our intention is to allow each of us a period of time in which to feel our way into the next step in our journey. We will reconvene same time, same place in thirty days. I will send an email to all of you with an agenda for that call.

The reasons for this shift in course are multiple. Several of our sisters have extenuating circumstances transiting large in their lives, challenging their ability to continue long-term commitment at this time. Others suffer from ongoing exhaustion and find any level of effort to be depleting. And while there are those of us who look toward continuing circle in a new, sustainable format, that effort can only be successful with a clear understanding of the level of commitment from the whole group.

Please take this time to sense how deeply you derive benefit from being a member of circle and our sisterhood as a whole. Listen for what it is that you would hope to gain or contribute by continuing to grow through this process. It is our hope that with this sabbatical, we will each be able to clearly feel the desire to resume our circle activities, or to know that our time to complete has come.

Should you have a desire to listen, share, or be heard during this time, please remember the foundation of friendship and trust we have created within our beautiful circle of women and call a sister!

This week, we will take the opportunity to share our thoughts and feelings as we enter into our upcoming thirty-day sabbatical.

Meditation: Thanksgiving

Relax into a comfortable position, slowly breathing in and out. Draw the subtle energy up your spine to the crown chakra and allow it to flow out the top of your head as you exhale. ... Repeat this several times to clear out your day, release your thoughts, and empty your mind.

Imagine it is late autumn. Snow is gently falling from a somber grey sky, and frost delicately coats the seed pods like hoarfrost as dying grasses whisper and sway in a chill wind. In their nakedness, the trees stand with their branches extended, noble and beautiful, leaves of deep red and orange strewn upon the ground, creating a colorful tapestry upon which you walk.

Dreamily, you make your way through the forest, suddenly finding yourself drifting effortlessly through a portal in time. As the light around you shifts to deep golden hue, you become aware that you are now wearing a beautiful festival gown, your hair long and silken, woven with flowers cascading down your back, your feet in slippers of soft pelt. As you walk along, you attempt to listen to the whispered conversations around you and finally understand you are on your way to a sacred ceremony of thanksgiving.

As you walk, the sun begins to fall behind the shadowed mountain peaks, throwing out a pallet of flaming colors that saturate the night sky and cloak the forest in golds and magenta and violets. You open yourself to the colored light, allowing it to be absorbed into your body until the moment of deep dusk arrives and the sun slips away for its night romp on the other side of the planet.

As a hushed group, you enter into a large clearing in the forest appearing through another crack in the fabric of time ... and finding your place in the circle, you recline on the soft ground and feel your spirit lift up from your physical form to begin its own journey. The night fills with chanting and voices singing in deep harmony, each with their own prayer of gratitude. You find your song of gratitude emanating from your own heart and pour it out into the night's symphony of melodic voices.

Through the flickering light, you notice a powerful presence in the center of your circle. She appears to be an ancient being whose depth of wisdom and ageless beauty has only increased through time. In her arms, she holds an immense sheaf of golden grain laden with bursting seedpods. She is surrounded by finely woven baskets overflowing with corn and peppers and all kinds of pumpkins and squashes as far as the eye can see.

She gazes around the circle with eyes that seem to glow with otherworldly light, affectionately acknowledging each of you. The energy of the clearing suddenly becomes enlivened with goodwill, good fortune, and thanksgiving. You can hear people begin laughing softly around you. You yourself suddenly feel giddy with joyousness at the knowledge that such abundance envelopes you like a magic spell.

Soon the entire forest cavern is filled with laughter, each of you exuding your gratitude and singing your thanks for the earth's generous bounty, her magnificent harvest once again. And with the laughter finally come tears of joy. As the tears fall from the happy faces and land on the ground, they transform into seeds, burying themselves in the earth's soil, planting a new crop for a new harvest, abundance begetting abundance, and so it goes ...

Still high from the endorphins, you begin walking back along the pathway to your home. Singing and dancing continue all around you, and the air is filled with a heady sense of festivity. Soon your family and friends will join you for this great celebration of gratitude, the Festival of Thanksgiving.

Sensing it is time to leave now, you gently tuck a promise into your heart, that you will always remember to give thanks for the generous spirit that watches over you, not just at harvest time but every day. (Pause.)

Remembering to bring your promise with you so that you can live it, you gently call your spirit to you and, united again, begin to travel together back through the portal in time. Gently ease yourself back into your physical body, slowly becoming aware of your surroundings … your candle … your room … your sisters sitting in the circle of light around you. I now place the talking stick in the center of our gathering. Let us share our gratitudes, our breakthroughs, and our intentions for our evolving sisterhood.

Closing Poem: The Late Autumn Darkness
(from poem by Rose Flint, Mother Tongue Ink, ©2013 from *We'Moon 2014 Datebook*)

> The late autumn darkness sinks its teeth into each day
> As the year's descent deepens.
> Shadows fill up the streets and cold creeps under the skin …
> Small valleys become bowls of mist, brimmed with endings—
> All the husks that held the bright fires of life.
>
> Listen for wisdom voices in the storm: Kali, Crow Woman, Ceridwen, Hecate—
> All know the need to cut and cull.
> This is the hour of the Cauldron of Transformation …
> And from Death comes Rebirth.
>
> In a world where women are disempowered:
> Denied education,
> Raped in war and in peace,
> Taught to distrust their own bodies ~
> Let the hag guide you to face down Fear.
>
> Do not get lost in grief!
> Ride your power! Disturb the air;
> Be the witch, the shocking voice of truthful stories that shatter the status quo:
> Protest,
> Refuse,
> Fight for a new equality that places the wellbeing of Mother Earth in the center.

The seven generations that will follow us are waiting, crying for a vision.
It will come from women, working together ~
Sisters, weaving their magic circles of intent.[77]

[77] Reproduced with permission from Mother Tongue Ink, Rose Flint, poem from *We'Moon 2014 Calendar Datebook* (Wolf Creek, OR: Mother Tongue Ink, 2013), ©2013 Mother Tongue Ink.

Closing a Circle—Step 2: Whether to Close our Circle - What We Have Found

Thirty days ago, we embarked on an intentional and experiential quest into the absence of circle. This week, we come together to share the fruits of our journey, the insights we have gleaned, the clarity we have derived from this lacuna … our time away.

Please come prepared to share your realizations and discoveries, your intentions regarding how or whether we shall continue to meet as a women's wisdom circle. In light of these new perspectives, we will make our way to our next true point of beginning.

To provide the optimal amount of time for this gathering, we will commence the call promptly, so please plan to be settled in and ready to romp!

Looking forward …

Meditation: Spirit Guides

Allow yourself to completely relax. Draw your breath deeply into your lungs, holding it there, and then exhale long and slowly, allowing the hustle of your day to be breathed out into the evening where it fades into the ethers … another day in the world drawing to a close as you enter your sanctuary where you dwell in soul time.

See yourself on your pathway. You recognize the familiar landmarks along the way, turns you have taken before, the trail well worn, layered with footprints you recognize as your own. These are the many paths of your earth walk as you have chosen to live it, and there is an abiding sense of comfort and safety as you walk along. Continuing on, you notice that the light illuminating your way shifts almost imperceptibly, and the plants and trees surrounding you vibrate with a new rhythm. There is a sense of safety still, but intuitively you know you have crossed over the threshold into unknown territory. There is a long moment when you wonder whether to continue on or to turn back … but soon you sense the presence of other beings farther along the way and cautiously continue moving forward.

Before you, a small lake gradually appears, surrounded by trees that soar far into the night, their branches stretching to the heavens. A new moon hides silent in the midnight blue sky, while light from a billion stars travels through space to skim across the water's surface, setting it aglow as if lit by an infinity of fireflies. As you gaze transfixed by the astounding beauty of the night, animals large and small, feathers, scales, and fur, begin to make their way out of the forest, winding down to the water's edge, and with them you see other women, each moving in close proximity to one particular animal as if they are the closest of friends. Reverently they gather by the water's edge.

Off to the left, you notice one animal waiting alone at the far end of the lake. Its eyes gaze steadfastly into your own, and you suddenly realize you know this animal. Since early childhood, it has been your spirit guide, your special companion. Eagerly you make your way across the clearing, and opening your arms wide, you embrace your old friend, pressing your foreheads together, feeling the transfusion of energy and light and the exquisite allure of ancient companionship, mutual trust, and joy. (Pause.)

Looking around, you now recognize the others as your sister travelers, all en route to new destinations, all united with their spirit companions. The memories of other adventures recall themselves to your mind, life choices from times past that have led you to this place and time, to the embarkation on this new journey.

With infinite trust and gratitude, you reach over and affectionately caress your spirit animal and, reassured, prepare to venture together into the unknown.

As your higher self moves confidently into the future befriended by spirit, allow your consciousness to return to the present moment in time and space. When you are ready, gently begin the process of reentering your physical form, adjusting yourself until you feel comfortable … and being centered and grounded, open your eyes, allowing them to adjust to the luminous glow radiating from the circle of women surrounding you. Welcome back.

Closing Quote: Homing
(Malanastar)

> They'd been on the road for longer than she could remember … more and more she found herself wondering, Where is *Home*? Yet despite the abiding weariness, a delicious tranquility wrapped itself around her like an electric current, warm and recharging. There was a luminous glow that seemed to emanate from the very center of her being—like a beacon illuminating her way. And with it, a steadiness, a sense of calm awareness that had seeped into her consciousness and become second nature. The others had noticed a new radiance in her eyes, and she'd seen it in their eyes too. Their vision had acquired new perceptiveness, an uncanny ability to truly see—not just in the sense of physical sight—*inner* sight. Their eyes were lit from within. Over the last several months, she had discovered

she *knew* things … didn't think them, knew them, whole. It hadn't to do with language or reason, it was a felt sense … a psychic knowing.

The group had expanded, one new member at a time, like threads woven into a tapestry. Some she had known before, but most of the travelers appeared along the way, fellow adventurers in the sacred jungles of time and space who seemed destined to join them. Guides and totem animals traveled with them too, mostly hanging out in spirit form, but every now and then, they'd show up big as life—romping and cavorting, laughing, growling, chuffing, preening—convincingly physical. One girl's companion was a red-tailed hawk who trailed the camp at a distance, flying in each evening to sit on the branch of a tree like a sentry, watching over the group with his piercing golden eyes. By dawn, he was gone.

They had traveled further than any of them could have foreseen, learning to communicate in new and different languages, rediscovering ancient rituals and customs, delving ever deeper into the mysteries of atman that continuously unfurled before them, luring them on. Together they'd forged the frothy rapids of self-growth and change, plunging down allegorical mountain passes and tumbling over craggy existential outcroppings until finally and gratefully coming to rest in deep green pools of water lying still beneath star-lit heavens … quintessential metaphors for the lives they were creating: the inner was becoming convertible with the outer.

The bonds that had been forged, their mutual care and camaraderie, was deep rooted and engendered a tremendous sense of inclusion, not only within the group but a belonging within themselves as well. She was coming together, becoming whole. Through the relentless push, she had excavated the brilliant facets of an extraordinary gemstone, the precious, audacious jewel that had turned out to be herself … and the proverbial eighty-four thousand doors had flown open in places no doors had existed, revealing choices she could never have dreamed. It was a different universe. She had witnessed her friends breaking through their own limits as well, emerging victorious and damp, like chicks who had doggedly pecked their way through the crusty shells that had protected them, confined them for so long, until finally the shell had to go. It took effort … and it was always easier not to travail.

But *being born*, the wildness of it, is a force to be reckoned with. It makes no difference if you have just mapped out the itinerary of your ideal life. The timing of coming home to yourself has its own rhythms, its own momentum. It cannot be negotiated.

Their sororal adventure had become their life, and they'd grown accustomed to relying on the group, buoyed in the sea of communal love. But the peaks they had scaled and the summits reached had been uniquely their own. Ultimately, she understood that this part of the journey, the soul's journey, is a solitary path.

Alone now at the threshold, she affectionately gazes back one last time to fix them in her memory, to wave, and to feel the boundless love—and then sensing the air currents eddy around her, gentle as the flutter of a hummingbird, she draws herself together and lifting her wings, steps forward, letting go into the light.

And so it shall be. Pass it on. [78]

---

[78] Reproduced with permission from Malanastar

Closing Circle—Step 3: Bringing Our Circle to a Final Close

I want to thank you all for the heartfelt call last week. It is just that kind of deep sharing that has defined our circle as the divinely magical vessel it is. To those sisters who were unable to be with us on the call, I am hopeful you were able to be there with us in spirit.

Because of the work we all have done these past five weeks and because of what we have discovered about where we are now in our lives and the choices we are making, this week marks the final call for the Circle of Deepening Light. I would hope, however, that it will not mark the final coming together of the sisters of deepening light. I encourage us all to continue to evolve our sisterhood in expanded ways. Let us take the many treasures we have received from this experience and, applying them carte blanch to our lives, practice the art of paying it forward.

Our journey together has been uncommonly good for the whole and has as well offered extraordinary growth to each of us individually and in wildly divergent ways. The process of completion will, I am sure, bring its own sweetness and teachings.

Come prepared this week to say bon voyage to each of your sisters with whom you have traveled this journey of transformation, and to receive their farewells in return.

Blessed be, beloved friends.

Meditation: Last Circle Meditation

Settle yourself one final time with your sisters surrounding you. ... Finding a position of comfort and peace ... allow your body and mind to come to a place of stillness. Allow any tension to move outward away from your body, to disperse into the ethers. Breathing easily, relax fully. ...

Visualize in your mind's eye, a circle—your favorite sort of circle. It could be the moon, a wreathe, a halo, a group of friends sitting around a bonfire. ... Whatever circle reveals itself to you, see it before you. Become aware of its form. Close your eyes and allow the circle shape to move into the space behind your third eye. Feel the power and the aesthetic appeal of its structure, the rounded, infinite boundary intrinsic to its nature. Notice the thoughts and feelings the shape evokes in you. (Pause.)

Now, move yourself inside the circle so you are contained fully within its form. Feel the circle encompassing you, embracing you like a protective oasis. You may sense your circle shift into a three-dimensional structure, surrounding you on the left, the right, above you and below you— like a sphere.

Sit within your circle or your sphere. Allow the ancient recognition of the familiarity of this space to permeate you. Breathe in the expansiveness, the protection, the mystical feminine aspects of birth and rebirth, nurturance and acceptance. Fill all your senses with the endless well of sustenance that exists here. … Bathe your mind in its stillness.

Know that circles are nature's gift to us as women. They provide for us a natural place to belong, to rest and recharge, a place from which we create. (Pause.)

Stepping out of your circle now, allow it to drift up and away until you can no longer see its form distinct among all the stars and planets in the night sky.

With gratitude, breathe a fond farewell and turn to see *this* circle, *our* circle, awaiting you. Welcome back!

Closing Quote: Find Your Pack
(Karen Moon, The Divine Feminine App: Find a Women's Circle, July 9, 2015)

Find your pack.

The past almost two years I have been hosting a women's circle. At the door to the Moon Lodge, we set down our roles and expectations and come together to honor life, the Earth, beauty, music, poetry.

We set intentions and share, not in a "bitch-fest," but as a means to keep walking forward and to realize that we all face obstacles.

It has kept me going through some very difficult days.

I have bonded with these women, and together we have created something magical … alchemical.

My mother fears that I have forsaken my Catholic upbringing and become a witch.

I know witches. They are my friends.

In fact, I relate to a lot of Paganism with its reverence of Mother Earth.

But I also like parts of Hinduism, Sufism, and many other traditions. I am no more a Pagan than a Hindu or a Sufi.

I am, instead, learning to be Myself. And figuring out exactly what that means.

Women's Circles are as varied as the rest of life. Some are open to new people, some are closed. Some are based on Christianity; some on Paganism or other traditions. Some involve yoga. Some are co-ed. Some involve singing, dancing, drumming, others are book studies or craft based.

There is one out there for you.

Find it. [79]

---

[79] Reproduced with permission from Karen Moon, "Find Your Pack," from *The Divine Feminine App: Find a Women's Circle,* July 9, 2015, Foxrivermamas.com.

Appendices

Example of a Guidelines Document

Where and when: Circle meets every Thursday evening from 6-7pm on a telephone conference line.

Commitment to Circle, timeliness, and attending to circle business ensure the development of enduring and intimate bonds among the sisters, fostering a vibrant and resilient network of support within the circle and without. It is important that you give yourself a quiet place, free from interruptions and multi-tasking for the circle meeting. To arrive at the meeting on time, fully focused for the duration, is a show of respect.

We understand the importance of authentic communication, to listening deeply as we speak our own truths, as well as hearing clearly the truths being shared by others. The levels of communication honed within a circle become a personal practice, a part of our lives that extends outward to our families and friends.

It is a woman's responsibility to do her personal processing outside of the circle meeting and bring positive and loving energy to each meeting. We are not a therapy group. The circle is about personal growth and practicing gratitude. During this 'living workshop' we will all experience blocks, fears, old patterns, etc. Sharing your progress is circle business; taking group time to work through your issues is not.

Privacy and confidentiality are of the utmost importance. Without them, there can be no safe place to reveal what we ourselves may not yet know. The circle provides a space unlike any other in our lives. It allows us to dive deep into our unfolding process. This can only be done with the acceptance and silent respect of our witnessing selves. Keeping circle business within the circle honors the dignity of the process of transformation.

To create a safe and sacred space in Circle, we do not promote our private businesses, services, or products, nor do we discuss politics or religion. It is inappropriate to record any circle meeting unless specifically agreed to by everyone attending the meeting.

The vision of Circle is about empowering each woman to learn to receive and to see her way to creating the life she desires. When we collectively focus our intentions on empowering each woman in our circle, and on being open to receiving that encouragement ourselves, we are doing exactly that.

Your circle experience will be what you make of it. If you choose to make Circle a priority in your life and support it fully, there is truly no limit to what you can accomplish and the benefits you will receive. Open your heart and step into the empowerment of Circle!

Reconnecting with Your Feminine Consciousness

- Understand the absolute importance of being true to your essential, most authentic self.

- Make knowing *yourself* and your *Self* your first priority. This will be an ongoing practice.

- Work to clear and balance your subconscious and unconscious responses. This will also be an ongoing practice, as the process of life will continually attach to you, shrouding and impeding your natural beingness.

- Understand what it means to be crystalized within your own being. Learn how to live an undivided life. Embrace whatever spiritual practices best serve you in this quest.

- Understand what the mind is and isn't. Come to comprehend the synergistic interrelationships of the mind, heart and gut, and to appreciate the importance of their alignment.

- Recognize when you are not centered or grounded; know the signs. Always enter into a relationship, activity, or project from a centered, grounded place.

- Seek outside support for yourself as a woman. This will be from other women who are engaged in and committed to their own evolutionary connection with the feminine consciousness, and the men who champion them.

- Know that women are the great keepers of the status quo. They will work tirelessly to bring the whole community up to the same level. They will also bring down a member who has risen too high above the status quo (tall poppy syndrome).

- Observe your own cycles. Understand the transient nature of age, stage and phase.

- Familiarize yourself with the archetypes.

- Know your tribe. Understand the stated and unstated values, rules, and goals of the group.

- Know that being a member of the group does not confer respect or protection to you. That can only be earned by your own ongoing nobility of character.

- Know the implicit threat that an empowered woman is to unevolved men.

- Undertake to comprehend the multifaceted threat that an empowered woman is to an unconscious, unempowered woman, and persevere.

- Recognize the many sources of inspiration, guidance, and support. Learn to *follow the teaching, not the teacher.* (Jonah Speaks Out, Universal Education Foundation)

- Honor the process of being a consciously evolving female as a lifestyle choice. Once the choice is made, you cannot go back.

Facilitator Resources and Materials

Circle leaders tend to seek out the resources with which they feel most familiar and comfortable. Books, articles, the internet, films, our mentors, even everyday events in our lives can all provide seeds for a topic, the material or inspiration for a meditation, a poem, or song. The sources and resources I turned to for inspiration each week were varied and generally chosen in response to the course of the circle itself, as well my own evolution and maturation as its facilitator.

I would like to express my thanks and heartfelt appreciation to the authors on whom I leaned for my own creativity and inspiration in guiding our circle journey. In many cases, I began with a core idea and then tailored its content and length to fit my needs. For example, most meditations were written to be eight minutes or less in duration, thereby ensuring the greater part of our time remain available for the group-sharing process.

At the outset, I had no conscious intention that the material would be used beyond our weekly circle meetings; the idea of passing it along in book form did not crystalize until much later. I have attempted to locate the original seeds of inspiration for the inquiries, meditations, and quotations included in this volume. The bibliography and footnotes that follow include all reference materials as best I could reconstruct. If there are omissions, they were not intended. Any alteration of source materials was done for applicability to our circle work, and/or for the need for brevity; no offense or disrespect of the original work or its author is intended.

Regarding Quoted Material and Permissions:

All permissions granted for the use of any quoted material included herein do not in any way constitute an endorsement of this work or the concepts, theories or ideas represented within it, nor does such permission imply collaboration with the author of any quoted passage.

Women in Transition and its author in no way claim authorship or copyright to any of the quoted passages in this book. Sincere attempts have been made to identify and credit all sources of borrowed work. If any of these insufficiently credited passages are your beautiful words, please contact me so you may be given proper credit. With gratitude and sincere thanks for the consciousness you teach, I remain in your debt.

Linda Laws
Boulder, Colorado 2020
https://womenintransitionunlimited.com

Book References

A New Earth by Eckhart Tolle (Penguin Group, Namaste Publishing, Inc.)

A Pearl in the Storm by Tori Murden McClure (HarperCollins)

Animal Speak by Ted Andrews (Llewellyn Publications)

Ask and It is Given: Learning to Manifest Your Desires by Esther and Jerry Hicks (Hay House, Inc.)

Astrology for the Soul by Jan Spiller (Bantam Dell Publications)

Church of the Dog by Kaya McLaren (Penguin Random House Publishers)

Creativity: Unleashing the Forces Within by Osho International Foundation (St Martin's Press)

Earth Prayers edited by Elizabeth Roberts and Elias Amidon (Harper Collins)

Eastern Body Western Mind by Anodea Judith (Celestial Arts)

Goddesses in Everywoman by Jean Shinoda Bolen (Harper Collins)

Goddesses in Older Women by Jean Shinoda Bolen (Harper Collins)

Grandmothers Counsel the World by Carol Schaefer (Shambhala Publications)

Medicine Cards by Jamie Sams and David Carson (St. Martin's Press)

Millionth Circle by Jean Shinoda Bolen (Conari Press)

Moving Toward the Millionth Circle by Jean Shinoda Bolen (Conari Press)

Osho Zen Tarot, the Transcendental Game of Zen by Osho International Foundation (St. Martin's Press)

Outrageous Openness, Letting the Divine Take the Lead by Tosha Silver (Simon and Schuster)

Pocketful of Miracles: Prayer, Meditations and Affirmations by Joan Borysenko (Warner Books)

The Artist's Way by Julia Cameron (G.P. Putnam's Sons)

The Book of Runes, Commentary by Ralph Blum (Harper Collins Publishers)

The Divine Feminine App: Find a Women's Circle by Karen Moon

The Elephant Whisperer by Lawrence Anthony (St. Martin's Press)

The Healing Power of Trees by Sharlyn HiDalgo (Llewellyn Publications)

The Prophet by Kahlil Gibran (Alfred A. Knopf, Inc.)

The Ten Top Things Dead People Want to Tell You by Mike Dooley (Hay House, Inc.)

The Universe Talks (www.tut.com) by Mike Dooley

The Woman's Book of Spirit by Sue Patton Thoele (Conari Press)

Transitions Making Sense of Life's Changes by William Bridges (Hachette Books)

Urgent Message from Mother by Jean Shinoda Bolen (Conari Press)

We'Moon Calendar Datebooks for years 2011, 2014, 2016 (Mother Tongue Ink)

Women Who Run with the Wolves by Clarissa Pinkola Estes (Ballantine Books of Penguin Random House Publishers)

Footnotes List

in Chronological Order of Appearance
(beginning with the first words of the quoted passage or its title)

[1] "We are one of the tens of thousands of women's circles …," Jean Shinoda Bolen, *The Millionth Circle* (Berkeley, CA: Conari Press, 1999), reprinted with permission of the author.

[2] "You will be teachers for each other …," Sherry Ruth Anderson and Patricia Hopkins, *The Feminine Face of God*, (New York, NY: Bantam Books, 1991).

[3] "Boldness has power …," from Johann Wolfgang von Goethe, public domain.

[4] "Actualizing our Vision," Sue Patton Thoele, *A Woman's Book of Spirit* (Berkeley, CA: Conari Press, 2006), reprinted with permission of the author.

[5] "A Connectedness Meditation" inspired from "The Anonymous String: A Meditation on Connectedness," 11/26/2000 by parish minister Richard Gilbert, reprinted with permission of the author.

[6] "A Guest House," from Rumi, public domain.

[7] "The Road Not Taken," from Robert Frost, public domain.

[8] "Like a magnetized needle …," Steven Pressfield, *The War of Art, Break Through the Blocks and Win Your Inner Creative Battles* (New York, NY: Black Irish Books, 2002).

[9] "Give Us What You've Got," Steven Pressfield, *The War of Art, Break Through the Blocks and Win Your Inner Creative Battles* (New York, NY: Black Irish Books, 2002).

[10] "If a little dreaming …" and "The voyage of discovery …," from Marcel Proust, public domain.

[11] "I have never understood …," from Lawrence Anthony from Goodreads.com, founder of Thula Thula Private Game Reserve, Zululand, South Africa.

[12] "Time and Space is where you chase things …," Mike Dooley, *The Universe Talks,* ©www.tut.com, reprinted with permission of the author.

[13] "Without this playing with fantasy …," from Carl Gustav Jung, public domain.

[14] "A Bee Story," from Robert Jaeger, reprinted with permission of the author.

[15] "Bhramari Breath Exercise," as taught by Dr. Vasant Lad.

[16] "The Soul languishes ..." and "I have worshipped woman ...," from Mahatma Gandhi, public domain.

[17] "Remember Who We Are," Melissa Myers, © 2012 Melissa Myers from *We'Moon* (Wolf Creek, OR: Mother Tongue Ink, 2014), reprinted with permission of the author.

[18] "Slave Driving Inner Mean Girls," Christine Arylo, reprinted with permission of the author.

[19] "But ask now the Beasts and they shall teach Thee," excerpt from the Sutta Nipata.

[20] "A Purification," Wendell Berry from *New Collected Poems*, (Berkeley, CA: Counterpoint Press, © 2012), reprinted with permission of Counterpoint Press.

[21] "Waiting with Truth," an excerpt from Shannon L. Alder, Goodreads.com.

[22] "Angels and Other Supreme Beings," Sue Patton Thoele from *A Woman's Book of Spirit* (Berkeley, CA: Conari Press, 2006), reprinted with permission of the author.

[23] "A Gift of Love," Mike Dooley from *The Top Ten Things Dead People Want to Tell You* (Carlsbad, CA: Hay House Inc., 2014), reprinted with permission of Hay House Publishing.

[24] "True Light," from White Eagle.

[25] "You are sitting down on a hill top ...," written by a Cantonese Woman from *Earth Prayers: 365 Prayers, Poems and Invocations from Around the World*, edited by Elizabeth Roberts and Elias Amidon (New York, NY: Harper One, 1991), page 386, reprinted with permission of the publisher.

[26] "Mindfully Listen," from E.C.R. Lorac, 1938.

[27] "You are not here to make things happen ...," Mike Dooley, from *The Universe Talks*, June 9, 2015, © www.tut.com, reprinted with permission of the author.

[28] "The things that have been lost to women ...," Clarissa Pinkola Estes, excerpts from *Women Who Run with the Wolves* (New York, NY: Penguin Random House, 1992), chapter 15.

[29] "What motivates you to change," Caroline Myss from *Caroline's Blog* July 2015, reprinted with permission of the author.

[30] "Financial Abundance," excerpt from *Abraham-Hicks* online, ©Jerry and Esther Hicks, AbrahamHicks.com, (830) 755-2299, reprinted with permission of the author.

[31] "Grandmothers' Meditation," from Holadia, reprinted with permission of the author.

[32] "Fairy tales, stories and myths ...," Clarissa Pinkola Estes, excerpts from *Women Who Run with the Wolves* (New York, NY: Penguin Random House, 1992), introduction.

[33] "The purpose of life …," from David Viscot.

[34] "Giving," Osho from *The Ninety-Nine Names of Nothingness: A Darshan Diary* (Zurich, Switzerland, Osho International Foundation, 1980).

[35] "Ho'o pono pono" from Dr. Ihaleakala Hew Len.

[36] "A craftsman pulled a reed …" and "God picks up the reed-flute …," two quotes from Rumi, public domain.

[37] "The Path of the Hero," Joseph Campbell from *The Hero with a Thousand Faces* (Princeton, NJ: Princeton University Press, 1968).

[38] "Ordinariness," Osho, excerpt from *Osho Zen Tarot, The Transcendental Game of Zen* (New York, NY: St. Martin's Press, 1994).

[39] "Everything Is Done in Circles," from Black Elk, Oglala Sioux holy man.

[40] "Gather the Women," Jean Shinoda Bolen, *The Millionth Circle*, (Berkley, CA: Conari Press, 1999), reprinted with permission of the author.

[41] "The Naming," Judith Duerk, excerpts from *Circle of Stones* (Novato, CA: New World Library, 1989), reprinted with permission of New World Library, www.newworldlibrary.com, preface, 32, 47, 85, 112.

[42] "The sacred and the sensual …," Clarissa Pinkola Estes, excerpts from *Women Who Run with the Wolves* (New York, NY: Penguin Random House, 1992), chapter 11.

[43] "When love expresses through you …," Osho, excerpt from *Talking Tao, Talk #1.*

[44] "If You Can Be Meditative in Your Sex Life," Osho, excerpt from *The Book of Wisdom: The Heart of Tibetan Buddhism, Talk #7* (Zurich, Switzerland: Osho International Foundation, 1984).

[45] "Release the Familiar" from Alan Cohen, BrainyQuote.com.

[46] "For a seed to achieve its greatest expression …" and "If you love beauty …," two quotes from Cynthia Occelli, Goodreads.com.

[47] "Learning from the Stones," Sue Patton Thoele, *The Women's Book of Spirit* (Berkeley, CA: Conari Press, 2006), reprinted with permission of the author.

[48] "Creativity and Crossbreeding," Osho excerpts from *Creativity: Unleashing the Forces Within* (New York, NY: St. Martin's Griffin, Osho International Foundation, 1999), Pages 169, 170 and 181.

[49] "Inguz, the 8th Rune: Fertility, New Beginnings, Ing the Hero God," Ralph Blum excerpt from *Book of Runes* (New York, NY: Harper Collins Publishers, 2000).

[50] "Let the beauty we love …," from Rumi, public domain.

[51] "You were born with potential …" and "Yesterday I was clever …," two quotes from Rumi, public domain.

[52] "But perhaps the most important lesson I learned …," from Lawrence Anthony, founder of Thula Thula, Private Game Reserve, author of *The Elephant Whisperer* (New York, NY: St. Martin's Press, 2009).

[53] "The message here is quite startling …," from Dr. Wayne W. Dyer, excerpt from his Introduction to *Ask and It is Given: Learning to Manifest Your Desires*, by Esther and Jerry Hicks (Carlsbad, CA: Hay House Inc. 2004).

[54] "As we learn to trust in the Laws of Attraction …," Julia Cameron, excerpt from *The Artist's Way* (New York, NY:GP Putnam's Sons, 1992).

[55] "Metta-Loving Kindness Meditation," Joan Borysenko, *Pocketful of Miracles Prayer Practice* (New York, NY: Warner Books, 1994), reprinted with permission of the author.

[56] "Often people attempt to live their lives backwards …," from Margaret Young.

[57] "Let's pretend, just for today …," Mike Dooley, *The Universe Talks,* April 1, 2016, © www.tut.com, reprinted with permission of the author.

[58] "We stand at the threshold …," Lisa Kagan, excerpt from "We Stand at the Threshold" from *We'Moon Calendar Datebook 2011* (Wolf Creek, OR: Mother Tongue Ink, 2011), reprinted with permission of the author.

[59] "Money helps us to help others …," Percy Greaves, Mises Institute of Economics (Auburn, AL, 1973),

[60] "Many people take no care of their money …," from Johann Wolfgang von Goethe, public domain.

[61] "Money is only a tool …," from Ayn Rand.

[62] "Power," J. Ruth Gendler, from *The Book of Qualities* (New York, NY: Harper Perennial, 1988), © 1988 by J. Ruth Gendler, reprinted with permission of the author.

[63] "Nothing Is Meant to Be," Mike Dooley from *The Universe Talks,* © www.tut.com reprinted with permission of the author.

[64] "My Symphony," William Henry Channing, public domain.

[65] "Embrace Your Bliss," Leena St. Michael, adapted from the March 8, 2016 International Women's Day in New York City, NY.

[66] "Don't Sit Still," Renee Hummel ©2006, reprinted with permission of the author. Renée lives in Colorado and can be reached at dreneehummel@gmail.com. She loves to share poetry that uplifts and inspires.

[67] "Silence Meditation," adapted from *Yoga Meditation,* Tripurashakti.com.

[68] "Setting a Cup for Shadow," Rain Crowe © 2012, from *We'Moon Calendar Datebook 2014* (Wolf Creek, OR: Mother Tongue Ink, 2014), reprinted with permission of the author.

[69] "More Than We Know," Rachel Naomi Remen, an excerpt from LivingFully.com, as adapted.

[70] "Possessions and the Extended Self," Russell W. Belk, an excerpt from *Journal of Consumer Research*, September 1, 1988 (Chicago, IL: University of Chicago Press, 1988).

[71] "I resolved to keep lightening my game ...," from Baba Ram Dass, excerpt from *Here and Now Talks, 1992.*

[72] "Where the Light Enters," from Rumi, public domain.

[73] "Tell Us of Pain," Kahlil Gibran, excerpt from *The Prophet* (New York, NY: Alfred A. Knopf, 1923), public domain.

[74] "When a butterfly is ready ...," Miss Ascentia from *We'Moon Calendar Datebook 2016* (Wolf Creek, OR: Mother Tongue Ink, 2016).

[75] "We delight in the beauty ...," from Maya Angelou.

[76] "Gardening is a form of prayer," Kaya McLaren from *Church of the Dog* (New York, NY: Penguin Books, an imprint of Penguin Publishing Group, a division of Penguin Random House, LLC, ©2000, 2008), pages 152–153. Reprinted with permission of Penguin Books, an imprint of Penguin Publishing Group, a division of Penguin Random House LLC. All rights reserved.

[77] "The late autumn darkness sinks its teeth ...," poem by Rose Flint, *We'Moon Calendar Datebook 2014* (Wolf Creek, OR: Mother Tongue Ink, 2013), reprinted with permission of Mother Tongue Ink.

[78] "Homing," from Malanastar, reprinted with permission of the author.

[79] "Find Your Pack," Karen Moon from *The Divine Feminine App: Find a Women's Circle*, Foxrivermamas.com, July 9, 2015, reprinted with permission of the author.

Afterword

An Individual Quest

Perhaps now is not the time for you to undertake a group endeavor. Become a virtual member of the Circle of Deepening Light and undergo your own personal transformation by walking your individual pathway with us.

- Proceeding at your own pace, consider each inquiry for several days or longer. Give yourself permission and the time to consider the topic fully, without limitations, evaluation, or critique.

- When you are ready, select a quiet, private space in which to process the work.

  Prerecording the meditation allows you to enjoy the fullness of the experience and will bring you to a centered, relaxed state.

- Using a journal or a voice-recording device as your talking stick, begin by expressing your gratitude and any breakthroughs you may have experienced during the week. Then share fully and truthfully whatever thoughts, feelings, and memories were evoked for you by the inquiry. As you share, do not censor or judge the words or ideas that may arise. Listen as openly and with as much acceptance as possible.

- When you feel complete, metaphorically lay the talking stick in the center of your circle and bring your time to a close.

- Give yourself space to digest and assimilate what you have discovered in your own sharing.

- You may wish to reread your journal or revisit the recording of your sharing until you fully comprehend your own words and have been able to integrate them.

- When you are ready, move on to the next inquiry.

You may wish to invite a friend or a family member to participate with you … but be aware – that's how circles are born!

This method may also be used to familiarize yourself with the sample circle material as you practice the art of leading a group. Whenever possible, speak out loud and listen deeply. Bringing your words into auditory reality gives you the opportunity to find your voice. This is an effective tool, both for mastering the skill of presentation as well as for empowering the intention of the message. Enjoy, and bon voyage!

Printed in the United States
By Bookmasters